Bible Dictionary

Gabrielle Kelly OP
with Joy Sandefur

Dominican Series

The Dominican Series is a joint project by Australian Dominican women and men and offers contributions on topics of Dominican interest and various aspects of church, theology and religion in the world.

Series Editors: Mark O'Brien OP and Gabrielle Kelly OP

1. *English for Theology*, Gabrielle Kelly OP, 2004

2. *Towards the Intelligent Use of Liberty: Dominican Approaches in Education*, edited by Gabrielle Kelly OP and Kevin Saunders OP, 2007

3. *Preaching Justice: Dominican Contributions to Social Ethics in the Twentieth Century*, edited by Francesco Campagnoni OP and Helen Alford OP, 2008

4. *Don't Put Out the Burning Bush*, edited by Vivian Boland OP, 2008

As a volume within the Dominican Series, this book represents one small strand in a long-woven and continuing cord of Dominican involvement in the advancement of Indigenous peoples in many places around the world. In this land, we recognise work with the First Australians, in Aotearoa New Zealand, commitment to the Maori, and in various parts of Asia, ministries with Indigenous and tribal peoples. We remember also the much-earlier prophetic engagement of Bartolome de Las Casas with Indigenous people of the New World, and Rose of Lima's identification with the suffering Indians of the Andes; and we salute also the work of many others in times and places unknown. The labours of all these, and those with and for whom they worked, are honoured in the publication of this volume.

BIBLE DICTIONARY

SELECTED BIBLICAL AND THEOLOGICAL WORDS

A LANGUAGE RESOURCE FOR ABORIGINAL AUSTRALIAN STUDENTS

Gabrielle Kelly OP
in collaboration with Joy Sandefur

ATF Press
Adelaide

First published 2008
Reprinted in 2013

ISBN: 9781920691936

National Library of Australia Cataloguing-in-Publication entry

Title:	Bible dictionary : a dictionary of biblical and theological terms / Editors, Gabrielle Kelly and Joy Sandefur.
ISBN:	9781920691936 (pbk.)
Series:	Dominican series ;5
Subjects:	Bible--Dictionaries.

Other Authors/Contributors:
Kelly, Gabrielle, 1938-
Sandefur, Joy, 1944-

Dewey Number: 220.3

Published by ATF Press
An imprint of the Australasian Theological Forum Ltd
PO Box 504 Hindmarsh
SA 5007

ABN 90 116 359 963

www.atfpress.com

cover design by Astrid Sengkey

Original artwork by WA Pickett, 2002, Darwin. A banner from the *Nungalinya* College collection depicting symbols of the Christian and Sacramental life. Clockwise from bottom left: the waters of the Sacrament of Baptism, the dove representing the Holy Spirit, the cross of Jesus and the human person enlivened by these gifts of grace. In central position are the symbols of bread and wine representing the Eucharist.
Used with permission of *Nungalinya* College.

FOREWORD

NUNGALINYA COLLEGE DARWIN

Combined Churches National Indigenous Education Network

Dripstone Road
PO Box 40371
Casuarina NT 0811 Australia

Phone: (08) 8920 7500
Fax: (08) 8927 2332
Email: info@nungalinya.edu.au
Web: www.nungalinya.edu.au

This volume, entitled *Bible Dictionary—Selected Scriptural and Theological Terms* by Gabrielle Kelly in collaboration with Joy Sandefur, has been compiled primarily as a language development resource for a particular learning community. This is the community of *Nungalinya* College in Darwin, an ecumenical college for Indigenous Australians whose students are drawn from traditional and urban communities around Australia. For many of these students, English may be a second, or perhaps even a third or fourth language.

Across the world, and within Australia, there are many people who need to learn in English for a variety of reasons, even though it is not the language of their hearth and heart. Students at *Nungalinya* College are motivated to this hard road of second language study of the Bible and other Christian books because they have committed themselves to serving Christ and teaching others about him. It is a hard road, made more difficult by the technical words they encounter throughout Scripture and in their studies. Many of these words are crucially important key terms that allow the special level of discourse needed when we speak about issues of faith and theology. There are words, for example, like Incarnation, or Resurrection, or Trinity; or seemingly straightforward words like Easter, Sacrament or Creed. All of these words are loaded with meaning, often pulling together stories and ideas from the whole Bible, or bringing into one word discussions that have preoccupied the Church since the first century. Even people who grow up speaking English have trouble with some of these potent and frequently occurring words. How much more demanding it is for native speakers of an Australian Aboriginal language, when their vernaculars do not have even a distant relationship to English or its linguistic and cultural ancestors.

As a consequence, students and teachers at *Nungalinya* wrestle constantly with the need for resources that allow the best chance for our students to understand the English they encounter. This *Bible Dictionary* will be of great assistance to both the learning and teaching efforts of our students and teachers. Constructed as it is—in word choice and sentence structure—to meet as far as possible the requirements of this learning community, the text together with the illustrations, in many cases done by the students themselves, will allow students at a beginning level with English to explore and master the building block ideas for talking about theology.

Because much of this text was trialled with *Nungalinya* students, we are confident that it will soon become a welcome resource in theology classes as well as for students studying at home. This volume also has the potential to become a useful language and learning resource in circles far beyond the limits of *Nungalinya* College and its sister institutions. It may even prompt further ideas for the development of useful resources in this particular learning environment. As one who has spent many years in the field of theological education among Indigenous communities, I wholeheartedly welcome the advent of this volume.

Rev Dr Steve Etherington
School of Theology, *Nungalinya* College, Darwin

CONTENTS

ABOUT THIS BOOK

This volume is first of all an English language learning and teaching resource. As a Bible dictionary incorporating selected biblical and theological words, it is intended to assist students and teachers of theology and scripture at *Nungalinya* College, an ecumenical training institute for Aboriginal and Torres Strait Islander Australians in Darwin.

Students at *Nungalinya* College come from many traditional and urban communities around Australia. They may face particular linguistic challenges studying in English, since English is often a second, if not a third or fourth language. While many Aboriginal people are gifted linguists,[1] this natural giftedness and capacity can more easily be activated with the help of suitable English language learning resources.

The idea for this book arose from discussions held at *Nungalinya* College in Darwin in December 2004, when a meeting was arranged to consider what type of English language resource might be useful to staff and students in the College's theology school. The idea for a dictionary of terms, in suitable language and format, and incorporating a significant artistic and pictorial dimension, was the outcome.

Compilation of the dictionary has been a lengthy process. Words for inclusion were selected by *Nungalinya* College staff on the basis of their occurrence within students' courses. A first draft was subjected to further revisions before being submitted for comment and suggestion to other key persons, including theological and biblical experts from the three participating denominations at *Nungalinya* College. The assistance of all these persons who gave of their time, thought and expertise is acknowledged with gratitude.

This book is intended to help bridge a gap for speakers of English as a second or third language. At the same time, it is recognised that there would be wider potential for its usefulness if it were to be translated into Aboriginal languages. As an eminent Christian church leader declared in recent times, 'the church ... in Australia will not be fully the church that Jesus wants ... until you [the Indigenous peoples of this land] have made your contribution to [the church's] life and until that contribution has been joyfully received by others'.[2] Hence, any moves to have this material presented through the cultural and linguistic lenses of those First Australians whose languages are in use would be welcome.

The definitions

This dictionary is an introductory resource for a specific learning context. We have therefore sought to provide only the most basic definition for each entry. While theologians and bible scholars from the participating denominations have read the draft and offered suggestions, there may be additional explanations and nuances which members of the different denominations may wish to add in their treatment of words. It is expected that, as a matter of course, teachers will provide whatever extension is deemed desirable.

It is important to bear in mind also the limits and the changing nature of language. Finding the most suitable words to speak the truth about God and the things of God is an ongoing task for theologians of the Christian community, because the mystery of God is ultimately not

1 See RMW Dixon *et al*, *Australian Aboriginal Words in English*, second edition (South Melbourne: Oxford University Press, 2006), 7. Multilingualism was often a consequence of the need to develop proficiency in the languages of neighbouring groups.

2 Pope John Paul II, Address to Aborigines and Torres Strait Islanders, Alice Springs, 29 November, 1986.

containable in any language. Moreover, words and their meanings change over the centuries, and as the Christian community constantly strives to move forward in its understanding, it finds new and better ways, more adapted to new times and different cultural circumstances, to express fundamental truths and beliefs. The definitions given in this volume are for the present time in the context of a particular learning community. Nevertheless, the explanations of words listed here are commonly those used in mainstream Christian churches at the present time.

Notwithstanding these necessary qualifications, this resource is offered in the hope that it will provide a useful tool as learners engage with the theology and bible content of their courses. If it were to serve as a bridge to further studies in these fields, we would be glad indeed! In any case, beyond the limitations of this volume, we trust in the power of God's word, read and studied in the light of faith, to achieve its intended effect in the hearts of learners:

> ... *the word that goes from my mouth does not return to me empty,*
> *without carrying out my will and succeeding in what it was sent to do.*
>
> [Isaiah chapter 55 verse 11.]

Gabrielle Kelly
Darwin, Northern Territory
October 2008

ACKNOWLEDGEMENTS

Resources used in the compilation of this Dictionary have been many and varied, and too many to list in detail. The following have been of particular value:

Arthur, JM *Aboriginal English A Cultural Study* (Melbourne: Oxford University Press, 1996).
Browning, WRF *Oxford Dictionary of The Bible* (Oxford: Oxford University Press, 2004).
Dixon, RMW, Moore, Bruce, Ramson, WS, Thomas, Mandy. *Australian Aboriginal Words in English.* Second edition (South Melbourne: Oxford University Press, 2006).
Freedman, David Noel, editor in chief, *Eerdmans Dictionary of the Bible* (Grand Rapids: Eerdmans Publishing Company, 2000).
Smith, Barbara. *The Westminster Concise Bible Dictionary* (Philadelphia: The Westminster Press, 1981).
Stanner, WFH 'The Dreaming' in *Traditional Aboriginal Society*, edited by WH Edwards, 225-236 (South Melbourne: Macmillan, 1987).
Woods, Laurie. *The Collins Dove Dictionary for Young Catholics* (Melbourne: Collins Dove, 1990).

Bible editions used

New Revised Standard Version. The HarperCollins Study Bible (San Francisco: HarperSanFrancicso, 2006).
The Jerusalem Bible (London: Darton, Longman and Todd, 1968).
Contemporary English Version. Holy Bible (American Bible Society, 2004).

The following persons are gratefully acknowledged for their valued contributions in offering suggestions and expert opinion on drafts.

Stephanie Nganjmirra, Christian leader, Anglican Church, Darwin.
Dr Denis Edwards, Catholic Theological College, Flinders University, South Australia.
Rev Dr Steve Etherington, Coordinator of Theology, *Nungalinya* College, Anglican Diocese of the Northern Territory.
Rev Jo-Anne Fulton, Coolamon College, Uniting Church in Australia, Flinders University, South Australia.
Dr Mark O'Brien OP, Catholic Institute of Sydney, Sydney College of Divinity.
Teachers and students at *Nungalinya* College who trialled a pilot version of this Dictionary in Semester 2, 2007.
Ms Dawn Cardona, former Principal, Maurice Heading SJ, former Catholic Dean, and Sister Mary-Louise Slattery FMM, Catholic Dean and Teacher, and subsequently, Acting Principal at *Nungalinya* College, who offered early support for the project.

The illustrations — art work, photographs and sketches — are integral to this dictionary. We thank all those who have contributed and who have given permission for the various works to be used. In particular, we thank many *Nungalinya* students whose works are included, M & L Joshua, Peterson Nganjmirra and those whose work appears as part of the Anglican Diocese of Northern Territory collection. *Nungalinya* banners remain the property of *Nungalinya* College.

We acknowledge the advice and sketches of Rosemary Yelland OP.

Photographs are mostly from various church communities in the Northern Territory.

Other illustrations are used with permission.

We also acknowledge the financial assistance given to this project by the Northern Synod of the Uniting Church, the Adelaide Congregation of the Sisters of Mercy, and the Australian Province of the Franciscan Missionaries of Mary.

We acknowledge with special gratitude the Australian Research Theology Foundation Incorporated (ARTF Inc.) for its generous grant towards costs involved in the production of both the pilot edition and the final version of this Dictionary. That assistance has greatly facilitated the realisation of this language project, in both its verbal and artistic dimensions.

LIST OF WORDS and CROSS REFERENCES

D

M

N

O

P

Q

R

Adoration

A

ABBA

Meaning: **An Aramaic word that means 'father'. Young children and grown children, as well as adults, used this word to talk lovingly to their father.**
Mark's gospel tells us that Jesus sometimes used this word to talk to God, who is as close as a father. Like Jesus, the first Christians also sometimes used this word to talk to God.

SEE ARAMAIC p 15

Examples: The night before he died, Jesus prayed in the garden of Gethsemane. *He said,* ***Abba,*** *Father, for you all things are possible; remove this cup from me; yet, not what I want, but what you want.*
[Mark chapter 14 verse 36.]

St. Paul wrote: *For all who are led by the Spirit of God are the children of God … When we cry, '***Abba***! Father!' it is that very Spirit bearing witness with our spirit that we are children of God …*
[Romans chapter 8 verses 14–16.]

What is the word in your language for God who made everything?........................

Talk about what you call God when you pray.

ADORATION

Meaning: **The loving praise and worship we offer to God.**

SEE WORSHIP p 279

Examples: We **adore** God by being grateful for God's love for us, by living good lives, by loving other people, and by worshipping with other people.

John the apostle had a vision of all creatures giving **adoration** to the Lamb: *Then I heard every creature in heaven and on earth and under the earth and in the sea … singing, "To the one seated on the throne and to the Lamb be blessing and honour and glory and might forever and ever!" And the four living creatures said, 'Amen!' And the elders fell down and worshipped.*
[Revelation chapter 5 verses 13–14.]

Is there a word like **adoration** in your language?..

<u>Advent</u> includes the four weeks before Christmas

ADULTERY

Meaning: **Sexual relations between a married person and someone who is not that person's husband or wife is called adultery.**

Example: *You shall not commit **adultery**.* [Exodus chapter 20 verse 14.]

What is the word for **adultery** in your language?..

Talk about the way **adultery** hurts families and communities.

ADVENT

Meaning: **An advent is when somebody or something arrives.**

Advent is the name of the season in the Church's year when we get ready to remember the 'coming' of Jesus at Christmas, and look forward to his coming again.
Advent is the first season of the Church's year. It includes the four weeks before Christmas.

SEE LITURGICAL YEAR p 157

Examples: The **advent** of alcohol brought great damage to traditional communities.

The first Sunday of **Advent** is usually late in November.

Advent is a time of prayer to prepare for the anniversary of the coming of God's gift to the world, Jesus Christ.

Do you have special times of celebrating the coming of something in your community?

ALLELUIA (also spelt 'Hallelujah')

Meaning: **A word we use when we want to praise God. It is a Hebrew word which means 'Praise be to God!'**

Example: At Easter time, Christians sing many **alleluia** songs, because they are happy that Jesus is risen from the dead.

Is there a word like **alleluia** in your language?..

Talk about the times you were so happy you wanted to say **'Alleluia!'.**

Altar
New Testament

ALTAR - OLD TESTAMENT

Meaning: **For the Israelites, the altar was the place where they killed animals and offered them to God. They also offered to God wine, corn and other gifts.**

The altar was outside in the open air. It was made of large stones, but sometimes heaps of earth.
Sometimes the altar was a place high up on a rock or hill.

Examples: The Israelites used to offer their sacrifices of animals to God by putting them on an **altar.** [Exodus chapter 20 verse 24.]

For the Israelites, their most important **altar** was in the temple in Jerusalem.

ALTAR - NEW TESTAMENT

Meaning: **In Christian churches, the table, often made of wood or stone, at the front of the church. In some churches, this is also called the Communion Table.**

This is where the priest or minister stands to make the people's offering to God.

Example: In many Christian churches, the people celebrate Communion or Eucharist by putting bread and wine on the **altar.**

Talk about what the **altar** looks like in your church.

Angel

AMEN

Meaning: **Amen means, 'Yes, it is true', or 'I agree'. It is a Hebrew word, and we usually say it at the end of a prayer to show that we agree with the prayer.**

Examples: *Our father in heaven, hallowed be your name. Your kingdom come.*
Your will be done, on earth as it is in heaven.
Give us this day our daily bread.
And forgive us our debts,
As we also have forgiven our debtors.
And do not bring us to the time of trial,
but rescue us from the evil one. [Matthew chapter 6 verses 9–13.]
Amen.

I knew he had finished praying when he said **'Amen.'**

In your language, how do you say: Yes, I agree! Is there one word for it, or more than one word? ....

ANGEL

Meaning: **A spirit messenger from God to people.**

Examples: The **angel** Gabriel brought a message to Mary that she would have a child named Jesus. [Luke chapter 1 verse 26.]

After Jesus was tempted in the wilderness, the devil left him, and **angels** appeared and looked after him. [Matthew chapter 4 verse 11.]

Is there a word like **angel** in your language?..

Talk about what people in your community think about **angels**.

Annunciation

ANNUNCIATION

Meaning: **The name of the story in the gospel of Luke when the Angel Gabriel gave a message to Mary that she would give birth to a special child.** **[Luke chapter 1 verses 26–35.]**

Examples: Many Christian Churches remember the **Annunciation** every year on 25 March, 9 months before the birth of Jesus.

Some Churches remember the **Annunciation** story at Christmas time, the birth of Jesus.

Have you ever seen a picture of the **Annunciation**? Talk about what was in the picture.

ANOINT

Meaning: **To ask the Holy Spirit to bless a person by rubbing them with holy oil.**

SEE CHRIST p 45 MESSIAH p 169 SACRAMENT p 233

Examples: In the Old Testament, people with a special job like kings and priests were **anointed** with oil. The prophet Samuel **anointed** David with oil to show that one day he would be King of Israel. [1 Samuel chapter 16 verses 12–13.]

If a person is sick, the priest may **anoint** the eyes, ears, nose, mouth, and hands of the sick person with holy oil. For Catholics, this is called the Sacrament of Anointing of the Sick. Other churches anoint the forehead.
[James chapter 5 verses 14–15.]

Is there a word like **anoint** in your language?..

Talk about a time when you saw somebody **anointed.**

Tobit
Judith
Esther

Wisdom of Solomon
Ecclesiasticus, or the Wisdom of Jesus Son of Sirach
Baruch
The Letter of Jeremiah
The Additions to the Book of Daniel
  The Prayer of Azariah and the Song of the Three Jews
  Susanna
  Bel and the Dragon
1 Maccabees
2 Maccabees

Apocrypha

ANTICHRIST

Meaning: **A figure or strong enemy who acts against Jesus Christ. [Anti means to be against something, eg anti-nuclear, anti-smoking.]**

Example: *Children, it is the last hour! As you have heard that* ***antichrist*** *is coming, so now many* ***antichrists*** *have come.*
[1 John chapter 2 verse 18.]

APOCRYPHA -SOMETIMES CALLED APOCRYPHAL BOOKS

Meaning: **A Greek word that means things that are hidden away. Apocrypha are very old religious writings of the Jews which are not included in the Bible.**

Old religious writings of the early Christians which are not included in the Bible are called Early Christian Apocrypha.

Note: **Christian churches have different opinions about which books should be included or left out of the Apocrypha.**

Example: The Old Testament books of Tobit, Judith and Esther, and some others, are considered to be **apocryphal books** by some Christian churches.

M & L Joshua

The Twelve Apostles

APOSTLE

Meaning: **Apostle is from a Greek word which means someone sent as a messenger with authority. Peter, James and John were apostles. They were witnesses to the risen Christ.**

In the gospels, the first apostles were the twelve called by Jesus. Jesus himself put them in charge of teaching the Good news to everybody. Later, Paul and others were apostles.

Example: Jesus went out into the hills to pray:
And he spent the night in prayer to God. And when day came, he called his disciples and chose twelve of them, whom he also named ***'apostles'***. [Luke chapter 6 verses 12–13.]

How do you say in your language, 'someone who is sent with a special message'?
……………………………………………………………………………………..

What are the names of the twelve **apostles** Jesus called to spread his message? [Read Luke chapter 6 verse 13.]

ARAMAIC

Meaning: **The name of the language spoken by Jesus and other Jewish people in Palestine at that time.**

SEE ABBA p 3

Examples: Some words in the gospels are not in English but in **Aramaic.** When Jesus prayed to God the night before he died, he said,
'**Abba** (this means God or Father), you can do everything; take this cup away from me … ' [Mark chapter 14 verse 36]

Jesus told the little girl who had died to get up and be alive again. He said, '**Talitha kum**.' This is **Aramaic** and it means, 'Little girl, I tell you to get up.' [Mark chapter 5 verse 41]

Find other words in the New Testament that are in **Aramaic** if you can……………………

M & L Joshua

Noah's Ark

ARCHANGEL or CHIEF ANGEL

Meaning: **A spirit messenger from God to people.**

Archangel is a more important angel, a chief angel.

SEE ANGEL p 9

Example: At the trumpet of God, the voice of the **archangel** will call out the command and the Lord himself will come down from heaven. [1 Thessalonians chapter 4 verse16.]

What are the names of the **Archangels** you know about?..................................

Look up these references in your Bible: Daniel chapter 8 verses 15–16; Daniel chapter 10 verses 13, 21, chapter 12 verse 1; Revelation chapter 12 verse 7; Luke chapter 1 verse 19; Tobit chapter 5 verses 4–8. What do these verses tell you about angels?

ARK

Meaning: **1) The boat which Noah built for his family and the animals to escape from drowning in the great flood.**
[Genesis chapter 6 verses 11–21.]

2) Ark (of the Covenant): The special sacred box where the Israelites kept the covenant tablets (the stones on which Moses wrote the Ten Commandments).
[Deuteronomy chapter 10 verses 1–5.]

SEE COVENANT p 59

Examples: When the Israelites wandered in the desert for forty years, they carried the **Ark** of the Covenant with them. It was a sign of God's presence, that God was with them.

The holiest thing in the Jewish temple in Jerusalem was the **Ark** of the Covenant.

Is there a word in your language like **ark**—a holy place where you keep something special?..

Talk about the different churches today—is there anything like an **ark**, a special holy place, in some of them?

Roman soldier wearing <u>Armour</u>

ARMOUR

Meaning: **Something that soldiers wear in war. In Old Testament times, armour covered their body like a shield—to stop a spear from hitting them.**

Examples: The Israelites put on their **armour** before they went into a fight.

When we fight against evil, St Paul tells us:
Put on all the ***armour*** *that God gives, so you can defend yourself against the devil's tricks.* [Ephesians 6 verse 11.]

What is the word in your language for a shield?..

What weapons does a shield stop?..

Talk about other kinds of **armour** you have seen.

ASCENSION

Meaning: **Something or someone going upwards. In the Bible, there is the story of the ascension of Jesus.**
We use this word to talk about when Jesus left his disciples and went to God after the Resurrection, 'Jesus was lifted up while they looked on.' [Acts of the Apostles chapter 1 verse 9.]
The church celebrates this on a special day called the Ascension. It is 40 days after Easter.

Examples: When they let go of all the balloons, they **ascended** into the sky.

Ascension day is a holy day for the church. It is when we celebrate the mystery of Jesus Christ going to God. [Luke chapter 24 verses 50–53.]

What is the word or words in your language for going upwards?...

Anglican Diocese of the Northern Territory collection

Atonement

ATONEMENT

Meaning: **To make up for doing bad things.**
To become one again with those you have offended (at-one-ment).

Examples: In the Old Testament, **atonement** was making an offering to God to show you were sorry for the wrong things you had done so that you could be forgiven.

On the next day Moses said to the people, "You have sinned a great sin. But now I will go up to the Lord; perhaps I can make ***atonement*** *for your sin."* [Exodus chapter 32 verse 30.]

In the Letter to the Hebrews we read: *Therefore (Jesus) had to become like his brothers and sisters in every respect, so that he might be a merciful and faithful high priest in the service of God, to make a sacrifice of* **atonement** for the sins of the people. [Hebrews chapter 2 verse 17.]

In your language, how do you say people who were enemies become friends again?

....

Talk about how people in Australia make up for the bad things they have done.
How do people in your communities make up for the bad things they have done?

Peterson Nganjmirra

Baptise

B

BAAL

Meaning: **The name of an idol, or false god, worshipped by the people of Canaan. The Canaanite people believed that Baal looked after the food crops they grew.**

Example: The Old Testament prophets told the people not to worship **Baal**, but only the one true God, Yahweh. [1 Kings chapter 18 verses 18–29.] [See also Judges chapter 2 verses 11–14.]

Is there a word in your language for a god like **Baal** who is not the true God?....................

Talk about what can happen when people worship a god who is not the one true God.

BAPTISE

Meaning: **A religious ceremony when a person is blessed, usually with the pouring of water on the forehead. This is the sign that a person becomes a Christian and member of the church, starting a new life by turning to Jesus Christ.**

In the time of Jesus, people were baptised by going right under the water. [See Matthew chapter 3 verse 16.]
In some churches today, people are baptised by going right under the water in a billabong or a river.
Baptism is the Sacrament of Christian Initiation.

SEE SACRAMENT p 233

Examples: *Then Jesus came from Galilee to John at the Jordan, to be* ***baptised*** *by him.* [Matthew chapter 3 verse 13.]

After hearing about Jesus, the Ethiopian said: *"Look, here is some water. Why can't I be* ***baptised****?" He ordered the chariot to stop. Then they both went down into the water, and Philip* ***baptised*** *him.* [Acts chapter 8 verses 36–38.]
Sally asked the priest or minister to **baptise** her as a Christian.

Is there a word or an idea in your language that means something like **baptism**?................

Talk about some initiations or **baptisms** that you have seen. Talk about what the water means in this ceremony.

Beatitudes

BEAST

Meaning: **An animal, usually a large or wild one.**
God made the wild animals of the earth of every kind - and God saw that they were good. [Genesis chapter 1 verse 25.]

Example: In the Genesis story, we read that God created every kind of living creature, - cattle, reptiles and every kind of wild **beast.**
[Genesis chapter 1 verse 24.]

Name some Australian **beasts** you know..

BEATITUDES SOMETIMES CALLED BLESSINGS

Meaning: **By remembering that God is with us always, we can be happy, even if life is sometimes hard and sad.**
Jesus told the people of many situations where they could experience these blessings. These situations are called 'the Beatitudes' or blessings. This is because of the words Jesus used in the gospel story. See the example below.
[Matthew chapter 5 verses 2–12.]

Example: *Blessed are the poor in spirit, for theirs is the kingdom of heaven.*
Blessed are those who mourn, for they will be comforted.
Blessed are the meek, for they will inherit the earth ...
Blessed are the peacemakers, for they will be called Children of God ...
[Matthew chapter 5 verses 3–5, 9.]

Read Matthew chapter 5 verses 2–12.
How many **beatitudes** are there?...

Talk about someone you know who lives like this.

Bishop

BIRTHRIGHT

Meaning: **The special rights of the first son born in an Israelite family. The special right was to receive the biggest share of the father's belongings when he died.**
[Deuteronomy chapter 21 verse 17.] **SEE FIRST BORN p 85**

Example: Jacob, the firstborn son of Isaac, was so hungry that he sold his **birthright** to his brother Esau for some soup. [Genesis 25 verses 34.]

Is there a word like **birthright** in your culture? ....

Talk about rights of the first child in traditional communities.

BISHOP

Meaning: **A leader of the church in a local area called a diocese. A bishop is ordained to be a sign of unity and to take care of the churches in a diocese.**
SEE ORDINATION p 187 DIOCESE p 71 MODERATOR p 171

Example: Anglican and Catholic churches have **bishops** in each diocese.
Some other Christian churches also have bishops. Other churches use different names for their leaders. [See 'Moderator'.]

Who is the **bishop** in your diocese?...................................

BLASPHEME

Meaning: **To speak badly or without respect about God or holy things.**

Examples: *And everyone who speaks a word against the Son of Man will be forgiven; but whoever **blasphemes** against the Holy Spirit will not be forgiven.* [Luke chapter 12 verse 10.]

That person **blasphemed** when he threw the Holy Bible on the ground and swore about God.

Is there a word like **blaspheme** in your language?............................

Talk about the way people sometimes **blaspheme** in your community.

Blindness

BLESS

Meaning: **To ask God to give health and happiness to a person, or to make something holy**

Examples: They asked the people to **bless** them when they set off on their dangerous journey.

In the Bible story, Jacob pretended to be his older brother Esau so that his father would **bless** him with the special blessing for the eldest son. [Genesis chapter 27 verses 1–29.]

Jesus told the disciples to let the children come to him.
*And he took them up in his arms, laid his hands on them, and **blessed** them.* [Mark chapter 10 verse 16.]

Is there a word like **bless** in your language?..

How do you ask God to **bless** someone in your language? What words do you pray?

BLINDNESS

Meaning 1: **In the body - not able to see**

Examples 1: Eye sickness can cause **blindness.**

Some people brought a **blind** man to Jesus and asked him to heal him. Jesus laid his hands on the man's eyes and his **blindness** was cured. He could see again. [Mark chapter 8 verses 22–25.]

Meaning 2: **In the mind – not able to understand**

Examples 2: The disciples asked Jesus why he taught the people in stories. Jesus said it was because of **blindness** in their mind and heart: *I use stories when I speak to them because when they look, they **cannot see** …* [[Matthew chapter 13 verse 13.]

Jesus said: I came into this world for judgment so that those who do not see may see, and those who do see may become **blind.** [John chapter 9 verses 39–40.]

What is the word in your language for **blindness**?..

Do you know of any **blind** people in your community?

Find some other stories in the New Testament where Jesus cures **blindness.**

Body of Christ

BODY OF CHRIST

Meaning:

1. **All Christians in the world joined together because they believe in Jesus are called the Body of Christ.**
2. **The sacrament of the Eucharist, when Christ is present under the appearance of bread and wine, is called the Body of Christ.**
3. **It could also mean the human body of Jesus, but is hardly ever used this way.** **SEE CHURCH p 47**

Examples: St Paul said: Now you together are **Christ's body**; but each of you is a different part of it. [1 Corinthians chapter 12 verse 27.]

And [God] has put all things under [Christ's] feet and has made him the head over all things for the church, which is his body, the fullness of him who fills all in all. [Ephesians 1:22–23.]

In some churches, when ministers give Communion during the Eucharistic Celebration, they say to each person, **'The Body of Christ.'**
In some churches, the minister says, '**We are the Body of Christ**.'

After Jesus died on the cross, Joseph of Arimathaea went to the governor and asked for the **body of Jesus**. [Matthew 27 verses 57–58.]

What is the word in your language for **body**?..

Talk about what it means to say we are together the **Body of Christ**.

BOIL

Meaning: **A very painful swelling that turns into an open sore on some part of the body. It is caused by germs.**

Example: In the bible we read that God punished the Egyptians with 10 plagues because they wouldn't let Moses take the Hebrew people out of Egypt. In the 6th plague, all the people and the animals got sick with **boils.**
[Exodus chapter 9 verses 8–12.]

What is the word for **boil** in your language?...

Has anyone you know ever had **boils**?

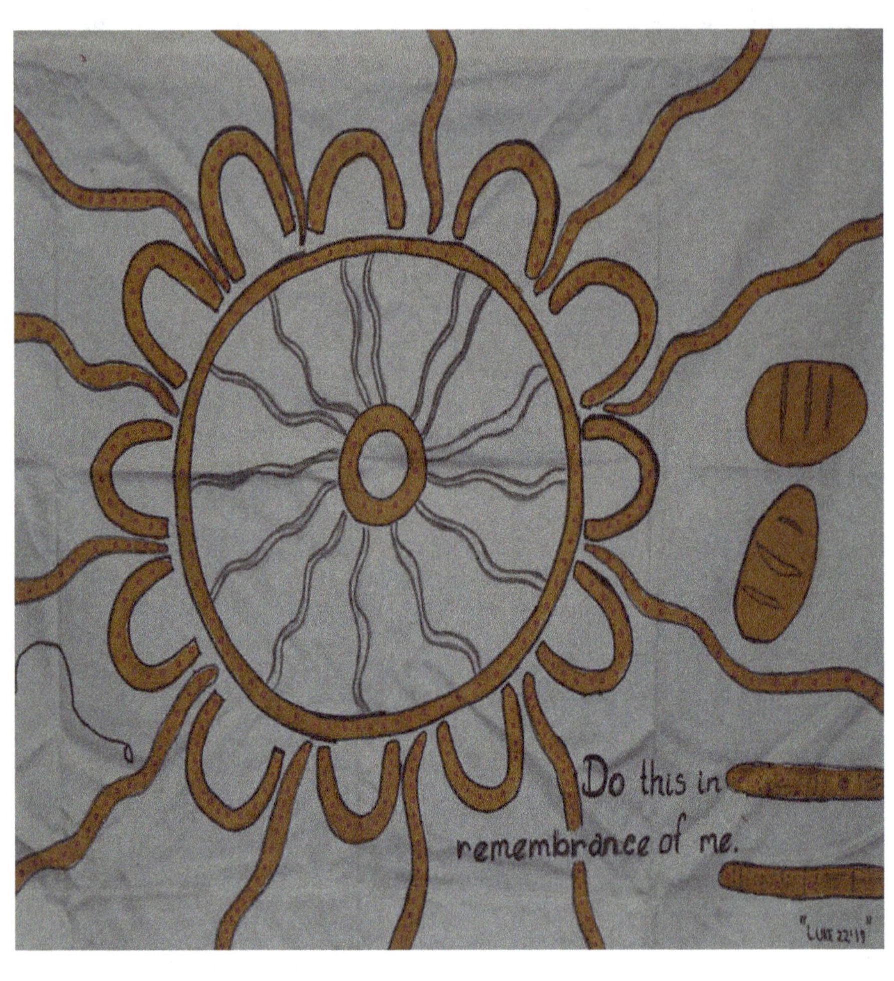

Breaking of Bread

BREAKING OF BREAD

Meaning: **The Jewish custom of taking a loaf of bread and giving thanks and praise to God at the beginning of a meal. Then the bread is broken up and shared among the people. [Luke chapter 22 verse 19.]**

What many Christian churches today call the Eucharist or Holy Communion used to be called 'the breaking of the bread' by early Christians.

SEE EUCHARIST p 77 COMMUNION p 51 LORD'S SUPPER p 159

Examples: Then [Jesus] took a **loaf of bread**, and when he had given thanks, **he broke** it and **gave it to them**, saying "This is my body, which is given for you. Do this in remembrance of me." [Luke chapter 22 verse 19.]

The disciples on the way to Emmaus only knew it was Jesus at the **breaking of the bread**. [Luke chapter 24 verses 30–31.]

Do you have a **'breaking of the bread'** custom in your community?

BRIBERY

Meaning: **To give somebody something secretly to make them do what you want. Or to receive some gift secretly for doing what somebody wants you to do.**

Examples: It is wrong to try to influence the decisions of politicians by **bribery.**

Sometimes, criminals who sell drugs try to **bribe** the police to leave them alone.

Through the prophet Amos, God told the Hebrews that they must not do the wrong thing, like forgetting about the rights of poor people, and taking **bribes.** [Amos 5:12.]

What is the word for **bribery** in your language?..

Talk about any time you know about where **bribery** has happened.

Burnt Offering

BURNT OFFERING

Meaning: **A gift of an animal offered to God as a sacrifice to praise or thank God, to ask for God's blessing, or to make up for sins. Parts of the animal were usually burnt on the altar.**

SEE SACRIFICE p 235

Example: Moses told the people how to prepare an animal for offering to God. After killing the animal and cutting it up, they burnt it on the altar fire. 'This holocaust will be a **burnt offering** and the smell of it will please God.' [Leviticus chapter 1 verse 9.]

A **burnt offering** was a ceremony for the Israelites. Is there any sort of ceremony like this in your culture?

Caesar

C

CAESAR

Meaning: **A name given to the ruler of the Roman empire. He was a bit like a king. When Jesus was born, the ruler's name was Caesar Augustus. [Luke chapter 2 verse 1]**

Example: Jesus said: 'Give to **Caesar** the things that are **Caesar**'s and to God, the things that are God's. [Matthew chapter 22 verse 21.]

Talk about the people today who are in charge of a country the way **Caesar** was in charge of the Roman empire. What name do we call them? ....

CAST LOTS or DRAW LOTS

Meaning: **To throw a dice or use some other chance way, like gambling, to decide something. The Israelites sometimes used this way to make decisions.**
It is like saying, 'heads or tails'.

Examples: Joshua wanted to divide up the promised land between the tribes. He said: *'Write down a description and bring it to me. Then I will **draw lots** to consult the Lord our God for you.* [Joshua chapter 18 verse 6.]

To decide who would have Jesus' cloak after he died on the cross, the Roman soldiers **cast lots.** [Mark chapter 15 verse 24
See also Acts chapter 1 verse 26. See also Psalm 22 verse 18.]

Do you do anything like this in your community?

Celebrate

CELEBRATE

Meaning: **To do special things for an important event. To have special ceremonies for someone or something.**

Examples: When the students finished the course, the whole college **celebrated** their graduation with a party.

Moses told the people God wanted them to **celebrate** together and to worship God:
These are the appointed festivals of the Lord, which you shall ***celebrate*** *as times of holy convocation, for presenting to the Lord offerings …*
[Leviticus chapter 23 verse 37.]

The apostle Paul encouraged people to **celebrate** the good news that Christ has saved us:
Therefore, let us ***celebrate*** *the festival, not with the old yeast … of malice and evil, but with the unleavened bread of sincerity and truth.*
[1 Corinthians chapter 5 verse 8.]

In many churches, every Sunday the priest and the whole congregation of people **celebrate** the Eucharist together. In most Uniting churches, the minister and the people **celebrate** Eucharist or Holy Communion at least once a month, if not more often.

Is there a word like **celebrate** in your language?..

Talk about some of the special events that you **celebrate** in your community.

CENTURION

Meaning: **In the Roman army, the soldier who was the boss of 100 soldiers.**

Example: In the Bible story, a **centurion** came to Jesus and asked him to cure his servant who was sick. [Luke chapter 7 verse 2.]

Is there a word in your language for the leader of a group?..

Talk about the different names of leaders in the army these days.

Ceremony

CEREMONY

Meaning: **When people come together for important sacred business such as initiation or a smoking ceremony.**

Examples: Churches have many different kinds of **ceremonies,** such as baptism, confirmation, Mass, Communion, funerals.

We read in the Bible about many **ceremonies** of the Israelites. For example, there was a **ceremony** for the Day of Atonement. [Leviticus chapter 16 verses 1–28.]

Is there a word like **ceremony** in your language? ....

Talk about **ceremonies** that are special for you. Talk about why they are special?

CHERUBIM

Meaning: **Creatures, with wings, from the spirit-world, like angels. Writers in both Old Testament and New Testament times said they worshipped God in heaven.** **[Revelations chapter 4 verse 8]**

Examples: When Moses was building the Ark of the Covenant, he told the workers to put two golden **cherubim** on the ark. [Exodus chapter 25 verse18.]

CHIEF PRIEST

Meaning: **The Israelites had priests who led the people in worship in the tabernacle and later in temples. The most important priest in the temple in Jerusalem was called the Chief Priest or the High Priest.** **SEE HIGH PRIEST p 113**

Examples: When the soldiers arrested Jesus the night before he died, they took him to the **high priest** whose name was Caiaphas. The **high priest** asked Jesus some questions. [Matthew chapter 26 verse 57 ff]

*Jesus is the **high priest** we need. He is holy and innocent and faultless ... he is better than any other **high priest.***
[Hebrews chapter 7 verses 26–27.]

Is there a word in your language for a special religious leader? ....

Talk about some of the names for religious leaders in your church.

Moses was <u>chosen</u> by God for a special task

CHILDREN OF GOD

Meaning: **In the New Testament the early Christians sometimes called themselves 'children of God' because they believed they were adopted as God's family.**

Example: But to all who received him, who believed in his name, he gave power to become **children of God**. [John chapter 1 verse 12.]

For all who are led by the Spirit of God are **children of God**. [Romans chapter 8 verse 14.]

With your teacher, talk about why the writer of John's gospel and St Paul might have called these grown-up followers of Jesus children.

CHILDREN OF ISRAEL

Meaning: **All the people who came from the tribe of Jacob (called Israel) were called 'children of Israel'.**
[Genesis chapter 35 verses 9–12.] **SEE ISRAELITES p 129**

CHOSEN

Meaning: **When a community chooses a person to do something (for example, be a leader, be a preacher), that person is chosen.**

In Old Testament times, God chose Abraham, Moses, David and others for special work in the community.

God also chose the Israelites for a special task of making God known to the world. They are called chosen people.

SEE ELECTION p 75

Examples: Two women were **chosen** by the community to study at *Nungalinya* College.

In the New Testament, Peter wrote a Letter to the community.
He said: 'You are a **chosen** race, a royal priesthood, a consecrated
Nation, a people set apart to sing the praises of God.
[1 Peter chapter 2 verse 9.]

How do you say in your language that God **chose** you? ....

Talk about the times when your community chooses some people for special jobs.

Christ

CHRIST

Meaning: **The Greek word for 'Messiah'. It means one anointed with the Holy Spirit.**
Usually, the king or someone special was anointed with oil.

In the New Testament, Jesus is often called 'Messiah' or "Christ" because his followers believed he was the special person promised by God from long ago.

SEE MESSIAH p 169 ANOINT p 11 JESUS CHRIST p 131

Example: When Jesus and his disciples were near the town of Caesarea Philippi, he asked them, 'Who do people say I am?'
Peter answered: You are **the Christ**, [Mark chapter 8 verse 29.]

Think about what you would say if Jesus said to you: 'But you, who do you say that I am?' [Matthew chapter 16 verse15.]

Talk about who Jesus is for you.

CHRISTIAN

Meaning: **A person who is a follower of Jesus Christ.**

Examples: There were many followers of Jesus in the city of Antioch, and it was in that city they were first called **'Christians'.**
[Acts of the Apostles chapter 11 verse 26.]

Paul told King Agrippa all about Jesus. King Agrippa said to Paul: Are you talking me into being a **Christian?**
[Acts of the Apostles chapter 26 verse 28.]

What word do you use for **Christian** in your language? ....

Church

CHURCH

Meaning: **'Church' often means the building in which Christians meet to sing, pray and worship God. But it has more meanings too.**

When the church started, 'church' was the Greek word for a meeting of the people all together.

Sometimes 'church' means all the Christians that meet together in some place. The Apostle Paul talks about the church at Corinth. [First Letter of Paul to the Corinthians.]

In our day, church can mean all the Christians in the whole world.

We also use 'church' to talk about the different Christian denominations; for example, all the Christians who are part of the Anglican church, or the Catholic church, or the Uniting church, or other churches.

Examples: A church that meets in one place:
From Paul … to God's **church** in Corinth … [2 Corinthians chapter 1 verse 1.]

A lot of churches together
The **church** in Judea, Galilee and Samaria now had a time of peace.
… The **church** became stronger as the Holy Spirit … helped it grow.
[Acts chapter 9 verse 31.]

Some Christian denominations or churches
Three different Christian **churches** are part of *Nungalinya* College today.

Talk about the different **churches** you know.

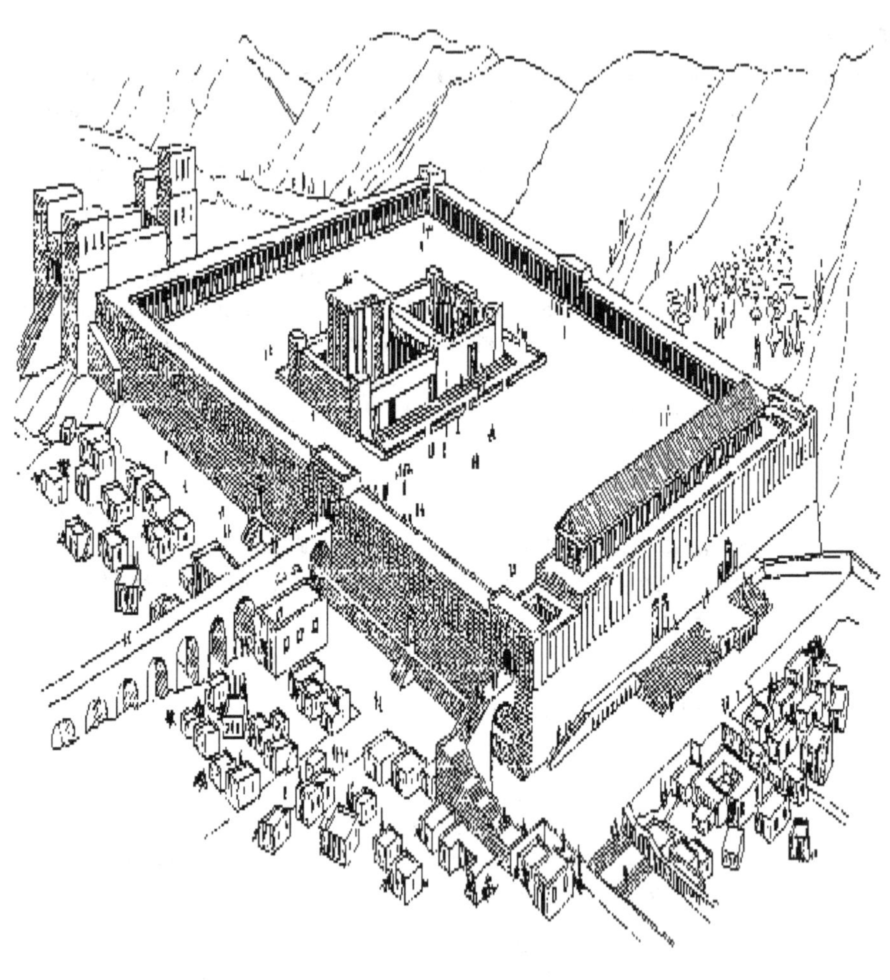

City of Refuge

CIRCUMCISION

Meaning: **The Jewish people used to cut away the extra little bit of skin around the end of a boy's penis. This was a special religious custom to show that they were part of the Jewish religion.**

Example: Moses told the people that on the 8th day after a baby boy was born, he had to be **circumcised.** [Leviticus chapter 12 verse 3.]

Some other people as well as the Jewish people practise **circumcision.** They have different reasons for doing this.
Does your community have a custom like this? What does it mean?

CITY OF REFUGE [Refuge means a safe place.]

Meaning: **For the Israelites, a place or a town or city where people could go to be safe from payback if they killed a person by accident. [Numbers chapter 35 verses 9–28.]**

Examples: *The Lord spoke to Moses, saying: Speak to the Israelites, and say to them: When you cross the Jordan into the land of Canaan, then you shall select cities to be* ***cities of refuge*** *for you, so that a slayer who kills a person without intent may flee there.* [Numbers chapter 35 verses 9–11.]

The person who accidentally killed someone had to stay in the **city of refuge** until the high priest died. Then he could go home.
[Numbers chapter 35 verse 28.]

Today, sometimes people in trouble go to a church to be safe. The church is like a **place of refuge** for them.

In your community, where can you go to be in a **safe place**? When do you need to go to a **refuge**?

Communion (Holy)

COMMANDMENT

Meaning: **The Commandments are the Laws that God gave to Moses.**

SEE TEN COMMANDMENTS p 261

Example: One of the teachers asked Jesus, 'What is the most important **commandment?**'
Jesus answered: The most important one is: You must love God with all your heart, soul, mind and strength. The second most important **commandment** is: Love others as much as yourself.
[Mark chapter 12 verse 28–34.]

Is there a word like **commandment** in your language?

Talk about what can happen when we don't keep God's **commandments.**

COMMUNION (HOLY)

Meaning: **'Communion' means becoming one with others.**
Holy Communion is when Christians share in the one bread and the one cup of the Eucharist in memory of Jesus.
They are made one with him and with each other.
Christians do this because Jesus taught them to do it.

SEE EUCHARIST p 77 BREAKING OF BREAD p 33

Examples: At dinner on the night before he died, Jesus shared the bread and wine with his disciples.
Then he took a loaf of bread, and when he had given thanks, he broke it and gave it to them, saying, 'This is my body, which is given for you. Do this in remembrance of me.' And he did the same with the cup after supper, saying, 'This cup that is poured out for you is the new covenant in my blood … '
[Luke chapter 22 verse 19–20.]

Some Christians have **Holy Communion** in their Eucharistic service of worship every Sunday (and on week days too). Other Christians celebrate the Eucharist less often.

Talk about when you have **Communion** in your church.

Compassion

COMMUNION TABLE

Meaning: **This is the table in the church where the priest or minister stands during the communion service or the Eucharist.**

SEE ALTAR p 7

Example: The bread and wine are placed on the **Communion table**.

What is the name for the **communion table** in your church?...............................

COMPASSION

Meaning: **Feeling for the suffering of people and doing something about it.**

SEE MERCY p 167

Examples: *In overflowing wrath (anger) for a moment I hid my face from you, but with everlasting love I will have* ***compassion*** *on you, says the Lord, your Redeemer.* [Isaiah chapter 54 verse 8.]

Jesus went away to a quiet place by boat, but when the people heard he was there, they followed him on foot.
When Jesus went ashore, he saw a great crowd; and he had ***compassion*** *for them and cured their sick.*
[Matthew chapter 14 verses 13–14.]

Is there a word like **compassion** in your language?...

Talk about some times when you have seen people show **compassion** for suffering.

Confirmation

CONFESS

Meaning: 1 **To say publicly to others what you believe.**
2 **To own up to doing something, usually not good.**
3 **To tell your sins and failures to a priest.**

Examples: 1 When Jesus asked his disciples who people said he was, Peter **confessed** his faith—he said Jesus was the Messiah. [Mark chapter. 8 verse 29.]

Sometimes at religious meetings, Christians like to **confess** their faith in Jesus.

2 Sally **confessed** that the lost book was in her room—she had taken it there to read.

When John the Baptist baptised people in the River Jordan, they first **confessed** their sins. [Matthew chapter 3 verse 6.]

3 Some Christians have a Sacrament called **Confession.** They **confess** their sins and failures to the priest and receive forgiveness from God.

What is the word for **confess** in your language?..

Talk about some experiences of **confession** that you know about.

CONFIRMATION

Meaning: **This is one of the Sacraments of Christian initiation, when a person becomes a Christian. When a person is confirmed, she or he receives the gifts of the Holy Spirit. This makes their faith stronger.**

Example: In some churches, the Bishop gives the Sacrament of **Confirmation** by anointing the person with oil and praying for the Holy Spirit to come upon them. In the Uniting Church, it is the minister who prepares the person for **Confirmation** and who confirms them in a special ceremony or service.

What initiation customs do you have in your community? What happens?

Talk about how your community celebrates the Sacrament of **Confirmation.**

Congregation

CONGREGATION

Meaning: **A large gathering of people, usually at a church service.**

Example: The **Congregation** at Church last Sunday was very big, because a lot of visitors came to celebrate a special occasion.

What is the word for a big gathering of people in your language?.....................................

Talk about what your **Congregation** is like.

CONSCIENCE

Meaning: **The inside part of me that tells me what is right and what is wrong.**

Example: When I do something that I know is wrong, I have a bad **conscience.** When I do the right thing, I have a good **conscience.**

What is the word for **conscience** in your language?..

Talk about what it feels like to have a bad or a good **conscience.**

CONSECRATION or CONSECRATED

Meaning: **A ceremony or ritual which marks a person or a thing specially for the service of God.**

SEE RITUAL p 227 ANOINT p 11

Examples: Dress Aaron in priestly clothes, anoint him with oil and **consecrate** him as my priest. [Exodus 40 verse13.]

When men or women are ordained as priests or ministers, they are **consecrated** for God's work.

When a church building is specially blessed to be a place of worship, it is **consecrated.**

Is there a word like **consecration** in your language?.......................................

Talk about the ways you **consecrate** things or people in your church.

Gertie Huddleston, 'Garden of Eden'. Anglican Diocese of Northern Territory collection

Creation

COVENANT

Meaning: **An important agreement between two people or two groups of people.**

In the Bible, the Covenant means the agreement that God made with God's people, such as the one at Mt. Sinai. God would be their God, and they would be God's people.

SEE NEW COVENANT p 179

Examples: God said, 'I am going to make a **covenant** with you. Before all your people, I shall work miracles. [Exodus chapter 34 verse10.]

God made a **new covenant** with all people in Jesus.
On the night before he died, Jesus shared the bread and the cup of wine.
He said: "This cup that is poured out for you is the **new covenant** in my blood." [Luke chapter 22 verse 20.]

Is there a word like **covenant** in your language?. ....

Talk about a **covenant** or agreement among two groups or people that you know about.

CREATION

Meaning: **The name we give to the story of how the whole world—the earth, sun, moon, stars, animals and plants—started and is able to go on.**
Christians believe that, however this happens, it is God who does it.

Example: In the Book of Genesis we can read a very old story about **creation** which the Hebrews used to tell.
[Genesis chapter 1 verses 1–31, chapter 2 verses 1–4.]

What is the word for **creation** in your community?....................................

Talk about some of the **creation stories** that your community knows about.

Cross

CREED

Meaning: **The early Christians wrote down the main things they believed about God, Jesus, the church community and life after death. This statement was called a creed.**

Example: At Church services, many Christians say the **Creed** together to show that they believe in the main Christian teachings.

What is the word for **creed** in your language?

Talk about the **Creed** that your Church community says on Sundays.

CROSS

Meaning: **Two pieces of wood fixed together at right angles. In the time of Jesus, nailing or tying a person to a cross was how the Romans killed criminals, slaves and rebels.**

Example: After the Romans arrested Jesus, they killed him by nailing him to a **cross.**

The **cross** is the sign for Christians everywhere.

Does your community have special signs? What do they mean?...................................

Talk about some other signs that Christians often use.

CRUCIFY

Meaning: **To nail a person's hands and feet to a wooden cross. This was how the Romans killed Jesus. This was the way the Romans killed people who rebelled against Rome.**

SEE CROSS p 61

Example: They led Jesus away and **crucified** him. [Matthew chapter 27 verse 31.]

What did your people do with bad people in the past?

Customs

CULTURE

Meaning: **The ways that different groups of human beings live in their societies.**

Examples: In Australian Aboriginal **culture**, family relationships are very important.

Sport is an important part of Australian **culture.**

In New Testament times, circumcision was an important part of Jewish **culture,** but it was not a part of Greek **culture.**
[Galatians chapter 2 verse 3; chapter 6 verses12–15.]

What is the word for **culture** in your language?..

Talk about some of the things that are part of your **culture.**

CURSE

Meaning: **To say the words that will make bad things happen to somebody. When people say the words of a curse, they believe that the words have power.**

Examples: They **cursed** the person who made trouble for them.

Micah's mother **cursed** the person who stole her money.
[Judges chapter 17 verse 2.]

What is the word for **curse** in your language?...

Talk about what can happen if a person is **cursed.**

CUSTOMS

Meaning: **The way people usually do things in their community.**

Examples: When Australians meet each other for the first time, it is the **custom** to shake hands as a way of greeting.

It was a **custom** of the early Christians to greet each other by saying, 'Peace be with you.'

What is the word for **custom** in your language?...

Talk about some of the **customs** of your community.

Altjerrele Kwerralye anthele.
ingwele akngenthe iletjeke.

Darkness

D

DARKNESS

Meaning: **Without any light, there is darkness.**
In the Bible, darkness can mean that God is not there.
Darkness can be a sign or symbol of sin and evil.
Light is a sign of God and goodness.

Examples: Night time is a time of **darkness,** specially when there is no moonlight.

When Zechariah spoke a prophecy about the coming of Jesus, he said that Jesus would forgive sins, and he would give light to those people who live in **darkness.** [Luke chapter 1 verses 77–79.] (This meant he would teach them the right way to live, as God wants.)

St Paul taught the early Christians that God took us out of the **power of darkness** by sending Jesus to teach us the right way to live.
[Colossians chapter 1 verse 13.]

What is the word for **darkness** in your language?...
Does **darkness** have other meanings in your community too?

When you read the Bible, notice how often you read about **darkness** and light.

DAY OF ATONEMENT

Meaning: **The day when Jewish people say sorry to God for the sins of the past year. They make up (atone) for their sins by praying and going without food. The Jewish people call this day *Yom Kippur*.**

In Old Testament times, there were ceremonies in the Temple on this day. [Leviticus chapter 23 verses 27–32.]

Example: The **Day of Atonement** comes on the 10th day of the 7th month in the Jewish calendar.

Is there a day like this for saying sorry in your community?..............................

Talk about some other ways we can say sorry for doing bad things.

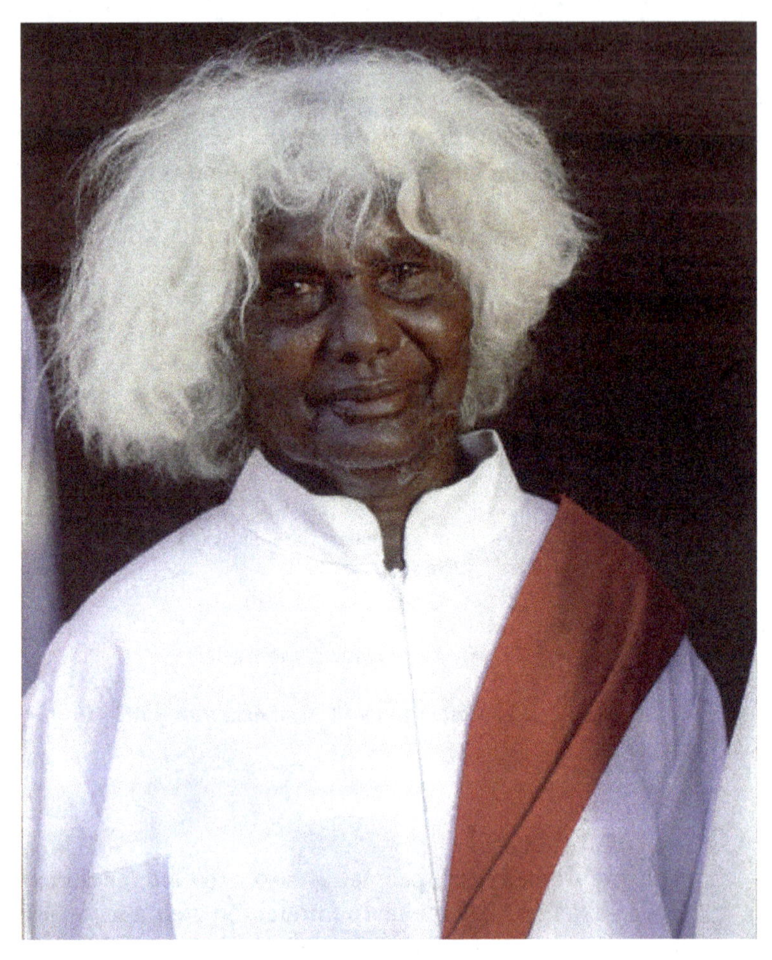

Deacon

DAY OF THE LORD

Meaning: **Prophets in the Old Testament used 'Day of the Lord' to talk about a day when people would know God and God would judge the people. They believed that when that day came, God would come into their lives to make all the people free from bad things. [Isaiah chapter 2 verse 12]**

For Christians in New Testament times, Day of the Lord means the final day of judgement for the world, when Jesus will come again.
[2 Corinthians chapter 1 verse 14; Romans chapter 2 verses 15–16.]

Example: And I hope that ... when **the day of our Lord Jesus** comes, that you can be as proud of us as we are of you. [2 Corinthians chapter 1 verse 14.]

DEACON

Meaning: **A person who is ordained to help the bishop as a minister in the Church. In the Uniting Church, a deacon is ordained to carry out special ministries of care and compassion for the poor and oppressed, and to seek social justice for all. Their ministry may be connected to one congregation or a group of congregations.** **SEE ORDINATION p 187**

Examples: The apostles told the people to choose some good and wise people to help them with God's work. They chose Stephen first. [Acts chapter 6 verses 3–5.] Stephen was a **deacon.**

Before someone is ordained a **deacon**, they need to study the Bible and things about God, they need to learn about the ministry of a deacon and be chosen by others to be ordained a deacon.

Talk about what **deacons** do in your church.

Jesus <u>delivered</u> Peter from drowning

DELIVERANCE or DELIVER

Meaning: **To be rescued or saved from something. Jesus came to deliver people from suffering and sinfulness.**

SEE LIBERATOR p 153

Examples: When the cyclone warning came, the people prayed to be **delivered** from danger.

At the last minute, the cyclone turned away from the city. The people thanked God for their **deliverance** from destruction.

When Jesus taught his disciples to pray, he taught them to ask God to **deliver** them from evil. [Matthew chapter 6 verse13.]

What is the word for **deliverance** in your language?...

Talk about some times when you or someone you know has experienced **deliverance** from something bad.

DEMON

Meaning: **In the spirit world, a bad spirit, sometimes called a demon or a devil devil.**

SEE DEVIL p 69 SATAN p 239

Example: When Jesus drove out the **demons** from two people at Gadara, they went into the herd of pigs nearby. [Matthew chapter 8 verse 28]

Is there a word for evil spirit in your language? ....

What do people say about evil spirits in your community?

DEVIL

Meaning: **An evil spirit.**

SEE DEMON p 69 SATAN p 239

Example: When Jesus got rid of bad spirits in people, some of the Jewish people said 'It is through the prince of **devils** that he casts **devils** out.'
[Mark chapter 3 verse 23.]

See further questions as for Demon above.

Disciple

DIOCESE

Meaning: **All the church communities of a Christian denomination in one region served by one bishop.**
In the Uniting Church, the area covered by a 'diocese' is called a synod, which is served by a Moderator.

SEE PRESBYTERY p 207 SYNOD p 255

Example: The **Diocese** of Darwin and the Northern Territory has its own bishop.

What is the name of the **diocese** that you belong to?..

DISCIPLE

Meaning: **A follower of a great teacher.**

Example: In the New Testament, disciples were people who followed Jesus, and lived the way Jesus taught them.

Is there a word for **disciple** in your language? ....

Talk about how **disciples** of Jesus live today.

DOCTRINE

Meaning: **Things the Church teaches about God and Jesus Christ.**

Examples: The first **doctrine** we learn is that God created us and the whole world because God loves us.

The **doctrine** of the Holy Trinity—three persons in one God tells us that God is a God of love.

DOXOLOGY

Meaning: **A prayer that gives glory and praise to God.**

Examples: Glory to God on high!

Glory be to the Father, and to the Son, and to the Holy Spirit!

Talk about some prayers for praising God that you know.

Elder

E

EASTER

Meaning: **The most important celebration in the year for Christians. It is when we remember that Jesus, after dying on the cross, got up from the dead into a new kind of life as the beginning of new life for all of us.**

SEE RESURRECTION p 223 PASSION p 191
LITURGICAL YEAR p 157

Examples: At **Easter** time, we have special Church services to remember the death and resurrection of Jesus.

Easter is a time to celebrate new life and new beginnings.

Talk about what you do during the **Easter** services and holidays.

ELDER

Meaning: **In Old Testament times, elders were the heads of families. Together, they were the leaders of the whole tribe. People respected them.**

In early Christian times, when the leaders of the local churches or Christian communities met together, they were sometimes called the elders.

Example: Jesus had gone into the temple and was teaching when the chief priests and the **elders** of the people came up to him.
[Matthew 21 verse 23.]

What is the word for people like this in your community?...............................

Talk about what the **'elders'**—the old ladies and the old men - do in your community.

God <u>elects</u> some people to do a special work

ELECT or ELECTION

Meaning: **To choose someone for something.**
The people who are chosen for something.

Examples: Every few years, Australians **elect** new people to be the government.

In the Bible, we read that God **elects** or chooses some people to do a special work for God. God chose Abraham to lead the people to the Promised Land. [Genesis chapter 12 chapter 2.]

All those who believe in God are **the elect**—the people chosen to praise God and to do God's Will on earth. [1 Peter chapter 2 verse 9.]

In your community, are some people chosen for special jobs?.......................................

Talk about these special jobs.

ETERNAL LIFE

Meaning: **A new relationship with God that begins with baptism, keeps on after we die and lasts forever.**

In the gospels it is sometimes called the kingdom of heaven or the kingdom of God.

Eternal life is given to those who live good lives the way God wants. Christians understand this means following Jesus.

Example: *Jesus said: 'Very truly, I tell you, whoever believes has **eternal life**.'* [John chapter 6 verse 47.]

Is there a word like **eternal life**, or heaven, in your language?...

Talk about the teachings in the bible about **eternal life.**

Evangelist

EUCHARIST

Meaning: **This word means 'thanksgiving'. When the church first started, after Jesus died and rose, Christians used to meet together for a ceremony called Eucharist or communion to remember him. Christians still do this today when they share in the one bread and the one cup in memory of Jesus.**
[Luke chapter 22 verse 19.]

Christians believe that Jesus is truly present with us as we share in the Eucharistic bread and wine. Christians have different ways of talking about how Jesus is present in the bread and wine. For example, Catholics speak of the "real presence" of Jesus in the bread and wine.

Eucharist is the ceremony when we say 'thankyou' to God for all God's work in making the world and sending Jesus to save us.

SEE COMMUNION p 51 BREAKING OF BREAD p 33

Example: Christians celebrate the **Eucharist** together in their church ceremonies.

What word does your church use for this ceremony?..

EVANGELIST

Meaning: **A person who tells the good news about Jesus.**
'Evangelist' comes from a Greek word which means 'good news'. It means the same as 'gospel'.

Example: Matthew, Mark, Luke and John—who wrote the four Gospels (the good news of Jesus)—are called **evangelists.**

Is there a word in your language for someone who takes good news to people?................

Talk about anyone you know in your community who is an **evangelist**?

How do you know if someone is a true **evangelist**?

Exegesis

EXEGESIS

Meaning: **Explaining what the words and sayings in the Bible mean for us today.**

Example: Some things in the Bible were written a very long time ago. The words are hard to understand. We need a teacher or lecturer to do the **exegesis** for us – so that we can understand better.

Talk about something in the Bible that a teacher helped you to understand.

EXILE or THE EXILE

Meaning: **An exile is a person sent away from their own country and living in another country.**

'The Exile' is the name given to a time in Jewish history before Jesus lived. It was the time when the Jewish people were taken away from their land after a war. They were taken as prisoners to the city of Babylon in another country. They stayed in Babylon for nearly 58 years. They kept their Jewish faith while they were in exile. When Cyrus king of Persia captured Babylon in 539 BCE (a long time before Jesus lived), he let the Jewish people go home again to their own land.

Example: A Jewish **exile** in Babylon was so homesick for his own land that he wrote a song. It is Psalm 137. It begins like this:

1 *By the rivers of Babylon—*
there we sat down and there we wept
when we remembered Zion.
2 *On the willows there we hung up our harps.*
3 *For there our captors asked us for songs,*
and our tormentors asked for mirth,
saying,
'Sing us one of the songs of Zion!'

Do you have a word in your community for someone who is not in their own land?......

What do you think it is like to be an **exile?**
Do you know anyone who is an **exile** from their community?

Exodus

EXODUS

Meaning: **A lot of people going out—a big mob going out from somewhere.**

In the Bible, Exodus is the name of the second Book in the Bible.

This book tells the story of how God helped Moses and the Israelites to get out of slavery in Egypt. This escape from slavery in Egypt is the most important thing that happened for the Israelites because it showed them how much God loved them. The exodus was the beginning of their history as a people.

SEE PROMISED LAND p 211 PASSOVER p 193

Examples: The Israelites remembered the **Exodus** when they got out of Egypt as a sign of God's saving love for them always.

Christians today remember the **Exodus.** It gives them hope that God will help suffering and oppressed people to become free.

Is there a word like **exodus** in your language? ....

Talk about some **exodus** happenings that you know about or can remember from your own life.

Fast

F

FAITH

Meaning: **Faith means we trust in God.**
It is a gift from God that helps us to believe in God and do what God wants us to do.

Example: Abraham had **faith** and obeyed God. He was told to go to the land that God said would be his, and he left for that country.
[Hebrews chapter 11 verse 8.]

Is there a word like **faith** in your language?..

Talk about what it means to have **faith** in God.

FAST

Meaning: **To go without food for a time. Christians sometimes fast for different reasons:-**

1. **as a way of praying;**
2. **to say sorry to God;**
3. **as a way of sharing what they have with others.**

Sometimes, people fast for their health.

SEE LENT p 151

Examples: In Old Testament times, the prophet Jonah told the people of Nineveh to **fast** and be sorry for their sins so that God would not destroy their city. [Jonah chapter 3 verses 1–9.]

Before he started his ministry, Jesus **fasted** for 40 days and 40 nights in the desert. [Matthew chapter 4 verse 2.]

For many Christians, it is the custom to **fast** during the Season of Lent, to get ready for God's blessing at Easter, to say sorry to God for sins.

Is there a word like **fast** in your language? ....

Talk about the **fasting** customs of different peoples.

Fellowship

FELLOWSHIP

Meaning: **When Christian people meet together they can have fellowship instead of an ordinary church service.**
Fellowship is a time of singing, testimony and prayer.

Examples: At *Nungalinya* there is great **fellowship** among the students and staff.

The early Christians enjoyed **fellowship** when they met together in their houses to remember Jesus and to share in bread and wine.
[1 Corinthians chapter 10 verses 16–17.]

Is there a word or an idea like **fellowship** in your language?....................................

Talk about some experiences of **fellowship** that you remember.

FIRST BORN

Meaning: **The child who is the first one to be born in a family.**
In some countries or tribes (such as the Israelites), the first-born child, especially the first-born son, received special rights. **SEE BIRTHRIGHT p 27**

Examples: In some cultures, the special right of the **first-born** son might be to get his father's farm and house when he dies.

Esau was the **first-born** in Isaac's family, but Jacob pretended to be the **first-born** to get his father's blessing. [Genesis chapter 25 verses 29–34.]

Is there a word or idea like **first-born** in your language?..

Talk about the idea of the **first-born** child having special rights.

Forgive

FIRST FRUITS

Meaning: **Every year, the first pieces of fruit and the first corn to ripen were not eaten, but were given to God. This was to show that everything belonged to God.**

Example: When you come to the land God is giving you ... you must set aside the **first fruits** of everything that you grow ... and offer them to God. [Deuteronomy chapter 26 verses 1–3.]

In the New Testament, St. Paul wrote:
... Christ has been raised from the dead, the **first fruits** of those who have died. [1 Corinthians chapter 15 verse 20.]

FORGIVE

Meaning: **To let go feelings of hate towards someone who has done wrong to us. To decide not to punish that person.**

But if that person has broken the law, they must still pay the legal penalty by paying a fine or going to jail.

When God forgives us for our wrong-doing, God wipes it away – like dew after the sun comes up.

Example: Jesus told his disciples they must **forgive** their enemy, not just one time, but seventy times seven times. We are to **forgive** many many times. [Matthew chapter 18 verses 21–22.]

Jesus taught us to pray:

> ... Give us each day our daily bread.
> And **forgive** us our sins, for we ourselves **forgive** everyone indebted to us ... [Luke chapter 11 verses 3–4.]

Is there a word like **forgive** in your language?..

Talk about a time when a person **forgave** you, or when you **forgave** someone. Is there still someone it is hard for you to **forgive**?

Freedom

FRANKINCENSE

Meaning: **The sweet-smelling gum from a tree that grows in Arabia. Some people used it to do magic.**

Example: Three wise men visited Jesus when he was born. They gave him gifts of gold, **frankincense** and myrrh. [Matthew chapter 2 verse 11]

Do you have sweet-smelling gum from trees in your country?...................

Talk about what you use it for?

FREEDOM

Meaning: **You can choose what to do. This is the first step.**

We truly have freedom when we are able to be fully the person God made us to be, and when we choose to love God and our neighbour.

Examples: In the book of Exodus we read that God helped Moses to lead the Israelites to **freedom** from slavery in Egypt. They were not slaves any more.

A person who is locked up in jail has no **freedom.**

The inside meaning of **freedom** in the Bible is that God makes us **free** from sin and death.

Through Jesus, God gives us **freedom** from our bad habits and the bad things we do, and **freedom** to live as God's daughters and sons.

Is there a word like **freedom** in your language? ....

Talk about a time when you had no **freedom**. What did it feel like?

Fulfil

FULFIL

Meaning: **To do what you promise you will do.**

Examples: After the cyclone destroyed their homes, the government said they would build new houses for the people. That's what they did.
They **fulfilled** their promise.

*Then Jesus said to them … 'everything written about me in the law of Moses, the prophets and the psalms must be **fulfilled'.***
[Luke chapter 24 verse 44.]

We read in the gospel that Joseph had a dream. The angel said to him: Mary, your wife, will give birth to a son and you must name him Jesus, because he is the one who is to save his people from their sins.
The gospel writer says: Now all this happened to **fulfil** the words spoken by God through the prophet. [Matthew chapter 1 verses 21–22.]

What is the word for **fulfil** in your language?..

Talk about some time when you have **fulfilled** a promise.

<u>Gabriel</u> told Mary
she would have a son ...

G

GABRIEL

Meaning: **Gabriel is the name of one of the angels. It is a Hebrew word which means 'one who stands near God'.**
[Luke chapter 1 verse 19.]

SEE ANGEL p 9 ARCHANGEL p 17

Example: **Gabriel** is the angel who told Mary she would have a Son … ' … *you will name him Jesus. He will be great, and will be called the Son of the Most High'* [Luke chapter 1 verses 26–38.]

Look up some other references to the angel **Gabriel** in your Bible: Daniel chapter 8 verses 15–26; Luke chapter 1 verse 19.

GENEALOGY

Meaning: **A long list of names of a person's ancestors—who was their mother and father, and who were their grandmothers and grandfathers for a long way back.**

Example: We can read the **genealogy** of Jesus in the first chapter of Matthew's gospel.

Is there a word like **genealogy** in your language?..

Why do you think Matthew's gospel starts with a **genealogy** of Jesus? What can we find out by reading a **genealogy**?

Write down your personal **genealogy.** How far back can you go?

Gift

GENTILE

Meaning: **In the gospels and in the early Christian church, anyone who was not a Jew was called a gentile by the Jews.**

Examples: St Paul knew that the work God wanted him to do was to tell the good news to the **gentiles**. [Galatians chapter 1 verses 11–12.]

St Paul told the **gentiles** that because of Jesus Christ, they were not separate from the Jews anymore; they were 'no longer strangers and aliens but … citizens … and … members of the household of God'. [Ephesians chapter 2 verse 19.]

What does your language call people who are from another place or speak a different language? …………………………………………………………………………………

What happens to people who look different or sound different in your society?

GIFT

Meaning: **Something you give someone free, for nothing.**

SEE GIFTS OF THE SPIRIT p 97

Examples: Many people give **gifts** on birthdays and at Christmas time.

God has given us the **gift** of Jesus, who shows us the way to live.

For the wages of sin is death, but the free **gift** of God is eternal life in Christ Jesus our Lord. [Romans chapter 6 verse 23.]

God gives people different **gifts** of the Holy Spirit. One may have the **gift** of preaching … another the **gift** of faith … another the **gift** of healing … and so on. [1 Corinthians chapter 12 verses 4–11.]

What is the word for **gift** in your language?……………………………………………………

What **gift** would you most like to receive? What would you like to give to someone?

Gifts of the Spirit

GIFTS OF THE SPIRIT

Meaning: **The special *abilities which the Holy Spirit gives to guide us. The Holy Spirit gives these gifts in the church so that people can help each other.**

There are many kinds of gifts of the Holy Spirit—gifts of prophecy,gifts of words,gifts of teaching,gifts of understanding, gifts of kindness and so on.

Examples: The **gifts of the Spirit** are love, joy, peace, patience, kindness, generosity, faithfulness, gentleness and self-control. [Galatians chapter 5 verses 22–23.]

God has given each of us different **gifts** to use.
[Romans chapter 12 verses 6–8; 1 Corinthians chapter 7 verse 7;
1 Corinthians chapter 12 verses 4–11.]

Look up the bible passages above—Romans and Corinthians. Make a list of all the gifts. Talk about them together.

What are the **gifts** God has given you?
With your teacher, talk about the fruits of the Spirit.

* Note: If someone is very good at doing something, like playing an instrument or singing or hunting, we say that person has **a gift or special ability** for doing that thing.

GLEAN or GLEANINGS

Meaning: **To pick up the small bits left over.**

Examples: Israelite farmers had to leave the grain or fruit that fell on the ground so that the poor people could come and pick up the **gleanings.**

'When you gather the harvest of your land, you are not to harvest to the very end of the field. You are not to gather the **gleanings.** You are neither to strip your vine bare, nor to collect the fruit that has fallen ... You must leave them for the poor and the stranger. [Leviticus chapter 19 verses 9–10.]

Ruth the Moabitess said to Naomi, 'Let me go into the fields and **glean** among the ears of corn ... [Ruth chapter 2 verse 2.]

Is there a word like **glean** in your language?..

Glory of the Lord

GLORY or GLORY OF THE LORD

Meaning: **The very great beauty and goodness of God present in all that God created—more than our words can say.**

Sometimes the glory of the lord is described as light.
[Exodus chapter 24 verses 15–17.]

In Jesus we see the glory of God in a special way.

Examples: *And as Aaron spoke to the whole congregation of the Israelites, they looked towards the wilderness, and the* ***glory of the Lord*** *appeared in the cloud.* [Exodus chapter 16 verse10.]

... *Moses went up on the mountain, and the cloud covered the mountain.* ***The glory of the Lord*** *settled on Mt. Sinai ... Now the appearance of* ***the glory of the Lord*** *was like a ... fire on the top of the mountain in the sight of the people of Israel.* [Exodus chapter 24 verses 15–17.]

Then the cloud covered the tent of meeting, and ***the glory of the Lord*** *filled the tabernacle. ... for the cloud of the Lord was on the tabernacle by day, and fire was in the cloud by night ...* [Exodus chapter 40 verses 34, 38.]

The heavens are telling the ***glory*** *of God ...* [Psalm 19 verse 1.]

In a vision, the prophet Isaiah heard the angels say:
Holy, holy, holy is the LORD of hosts; the whole earth is full of [God's] ***glory****.* [Isaiah chapter 6 verse 3.]

Mary and Martha sent a message to Jesus because their brother Lazarus was ill. Jesus said: *This illness does not lead to death; rather it is for* ***God's glory****, so that the Son of God may be glorified through it.*
[John chapter 11 verse 4.]

Is there a word like **glory** in your language?..

Glory is mentioned many times in the Bible. Look up some more references and talk about them. Eg Matthew chapter 17 verse 2 (transfiguration); Matthew chapter 25 verse 31; Luke chapter 2 verse 14; John chapter 1 verse 14.

Gods

GOD

Meaning: **The one and only creator and saviour of everything.**

'God' is the word for the Creator used by many English-speaking people. It is a word borrowed from another older language, because English didn't have a word for this. Other people may use different names.

SEE YAHWEH p 221

Example: In the beginning, **God** created the heavens and the earth. [Genesis chapter 1 verse1]

What are some of the names for **God** in your language? ....

Talk about some other names for **God** used by Christians and some names used by people of other religions.

GODS

Meaning: **These were the gods worshipped by the Canaanites and other people who lived near the Israelites. The people believed that these gods made the crops grow and the animals give birth. One of these gods was called Baal.** **SEE BAAL p 23 IDOL p 123**

Example: Moses told the people not to worship other **gods**, but only the one true God. [Exodus chapter 20 verses 2–3.]

Is there a word for other **gods**—not the true God—in your language?......................

Gospel

GOD'S POWER

Meaning: **God's power gives life to everything and every person, animal and plant in the whole universe.**

Example: *It is God who made the earth by **[God's] power.***
[Jeremiah chapter 10 verse 12.]

The people could see **God's power** in the healings done by Jesus: 'What deeds of **power** are being done by his hands!' [Mark chapter 6 verse 2.]

'... but we proclaim Christ crucified ... Christ the **power of God** and the wisdom of God ... ' [1 Corinthians chapter 1 verses 23–24.]

How do you talk about **God's power** in your language? ....

Talk about when you have seen **God's power** work in your life.
Have you seen **God's power** in someone's life?

GOSPEL

Meaning: **Gospel is an old English word. It means 'good news'. We use this word for the good news Jesus told the people about God.**

The stories which Matthew, Mark, Luke and John wrote about the life and teachings of Jesus are called gospels.

Examples: Jesus came to Galilee, proclaiming the **good news** of God, and saying, 'The time is fulfilled, and the kingdom of God has come near; repent and believe in the **good news**.' [Mark chapater 1 verses 14–15.]

The **Gospel** of Matthew begins with a list of all the names of the ancestors of Jesus.

What is the word for **gospel** in your language?....................................

Talk about what happens when someone believes the **gospel** and follows Jesus.

Mat 4 5 ἔστησεν (vl ἵστησιν) αὐτὸν ἐπὶ τὸ πτε-
ρύγιον τοῦ ἱεροῦ ‖ Luc 4 9 ἔστησεν
18 2 ἔστησεν αὐτὸ ἐν μέσῳ αὐτῶν ‖ Mar
9 36 Luc 9 47 παρ' ἑαυτῷ — [Joh 8 3
στήσαντες αὐτὴν ἐν μέσῳ] Act 4 7
25 33 στήσει τὰ μὲν πρόβατα ἐκ δεξιῶν
26 15 „ἔστησαν"[b] αὐτῷ „τριάκ. ἀργύρια"
(Mar 7 9 vl ἵνα τὴν παράδοσιν ὑμῶν στήσητε)
Act 1 23 ἔστησαν δύο, Ἰωσὴφ – καὶ Μαθθίαν
5 27 αὐτοὺς ἔστησαν ἐν τῷ συνεδρίῳ
6 6 οὓς ἔστησαν ἐνώπ. τῶν ἀποστόλων
— 13 ἔστησάν τε μάρτυρας ψευδεῖς
7 60 μὴ στήσῃς αὐτοῖς – τὴν ἁμαρτίαν
17 31 ἔστησεν ἡμέραν ἐν ᾗ μέλλει κρίνειν
22 30 τὸν Παῦλον ἔστησεν εἰς αὐτούς
Rm 3 31 μὴ γένοιτο, ἀλλὰ νόμον ἱστάνομεν
10 3 τὴν ἰδίαν (sc δικ.) ζητοῦντες στῆσαι
14 4 δυνατεῖ – ὁ κύριος στῆσαι αὐτόν
Hb 10 9 ἀναιρεῖ τὸ πρῶτον ἵνα τὸ δεύτερον

The New Testament was first written in <u>Greek</u>

GRACE

Meaning: **Grace is God's gift to us. It means God's kindness and love for us. What God gives us is God's self in love.**

Examples: The angel Gabriel came to Mary and said: Hail, you who are full of **grace.** God is with you. [Luke chapter 1 verse 28]

When Paul had a problem in his life, he asked God to take it away. Then he heard these words from God: *My **grace** is sufficient for you, for power is made perfect in weakness.* [2 Corinthians chapter 12 verse 9.]

The apostle Paul taught the people about God's great love for us, even though we have sinned. He said: *By **grace** you have been saved.* [Ephesians chapter 2 verse 5.]

Is there an idea like **grace** in your language?..

Talk about what it is like to know the kindness and love of God.

GREEK

Meaning: **The name of a person from a country called Greece. Greek was a language used in the time of Jesus.**

Examples: The New Testament was first written in **Greek.**

New Testament **Greek** was spoken by a lot of people in the Roman empire. It was a bit like Kriol—a lot of people from different languages used to talk to one another in **Greek.**

Guilt

GUILT or GUILTY

Meaning 1: **Being at fault for doing something wrong.**

SEE ATONEMENT p 21

Examples 1: If the courts and the magistrate decide a person is **guilty** of a crime, that person may go to jail.

Moses told the people if they did something wrong they had to make up for it: *You shall bring as your* ***guilt offering*** *to the Lord, a ram without blemish from the flock.* [Leviticus chapter 5 verse 15.]

The Psalmist wrote that when he confessed his sin to God,
God *forgave the* ***guilt*** *of (his) sin.* [Psalm 32 verse 5.]

Meaning 2: **A bad feeling that comes from doing wrong.**

Example 2: Those people knew they had done wrong by stealing.
They felt **guilty** in their hearts.

Is there a word like **guilt** in your language?..

Talk about what it feels like to be **guilty**.

Harvest

H

HADES

Meaning: **The Jews believed that Hades was the place where people went after they died. Some believed it was a place of waiting after a person died, before the judgement.**
This Greek word was sometimes translated into English as hell. **SEE HELL p 113**

Examples: In the bible we read that on Judgement Day, the dead people in Hades will be judged by God for what they did on earth.
[Revelations chapter 20 verse13.]

In the Creed we say: ' … Jesus was crucified and died; he descended into **Hell**; on the third day he arose again … '

Is there a word in your language for a place where people go after they die?......................

HALLELUJAH SEE ALLELUIA p 5

HARVEST

Meaning: **Harvest is a time when fruit is ready to pick and when corn and wheat are ready to be cut.**
[Deuteronomy chapter 25 verse 4; 1 Corinthians chapter 9 verse 9.]
SEE REAP p 217

Example: In the gospel story about the weeds in the wheat, the farmer told the workers to leave the weeds until **harvest** time. Then he would burn the weeds and keep the wheat. [Matthew chapter 13 verses 24–29.]

Is there a word in your language for the time when a lot of fruits and food are ripe and ready to be picked?……………………………………………..

Talk about what people in your community do at this time.

Hebrew writing

HEAVEN

Meaning 1: For the Israelites, heaven was the place above the earth where the birds fly and where the rain comes from.

Examples: King Melchizedek blessed Abram. He said:
Blessed be Abram by God Most High, maker of ***heaven*** *and earth.*
[Genesis chapter 14 verse 19.]

The word of the LORD *came to Abram in a vision …*
'Look toward ***heaven*** *and count the stars, if you are able to count them.'*
[Genesis chapter 15 verses 1, 5.]

Are you the Messiah, the Son of the Blessed One? Jesus said, I am; and you will see the Son of Man sitting at the right hand of the Power and coming with the clouds of ***heaven.*** [Mark chapter 14: verse 62.]

Meaning 2: For Christians, heaven is not a place but a different kind of life after death. Christians believe they will live forever with God in this different kind of life we call heaven.

SEE KINGDOM OF HEAVEN/GOD p 143

Example 2: *For we know that if the earthly tent we live in is destroyed, we have a building from God, a house not made with hands, eternal in the* ***heavens****. For in this tent we groan, longing to be clothed with our* ***heavenly*** *dwelling …*
[2 Corinthians chapter 5 verses 1–2.]

Is there a word in your language for life after death?…………………………….

Talk about some of the other everyday meanings of **heaven** in the English language.

HEBREW

Meaning: **1 Another name for the Israelites or Jewish people.**

2 The name of the language they speak.

SEE ISRAELITES p 129

Gambling
Fight
1
2
3
Money
angry
Jealous
Hate
VB
VB
Proud
Drinking

Hell

HELL

Meaning: **Hell is rejecting God forever. People who deliberately turn away from God cut themselves off from happiness.**

At the time when Jesus lived on earth, the Jewish people thought of hell as a dark place or a place of fire.
[Matthew chapter 8 verse 12; Matthew chapter 18 verse 9.]

SEE HADES p 109

Examples: *If you call someone a fool, you will be taken to court. And if you say that someone is worthless, you will be in danger of the fires of* ***hell.***
[Matthew chapter 5 verse 22]

And if your eye causes you to stumble, tear it out and throw it away; it is better for you to enter life with one eye than to have two eyes and to be thrown into the ***hell of fire****.* [Matthew chapter 18 verse 9.]

Is there a word like **hell** in your language?..

HERESY

Meaning: **In the church, a heresy is a false teaching.**

Example: Peter warned the people that just as there were false prophets in the past, so too there could be false teachers today. The false teachings would be **heresy**. [2 Peter 2:1.]

Is there a word for wrong teaching in your language?..

Talk about what happens if wrong teaching comes to your church or community.

HIGH PRIEST — SEE CHIEF PRIEST p 41

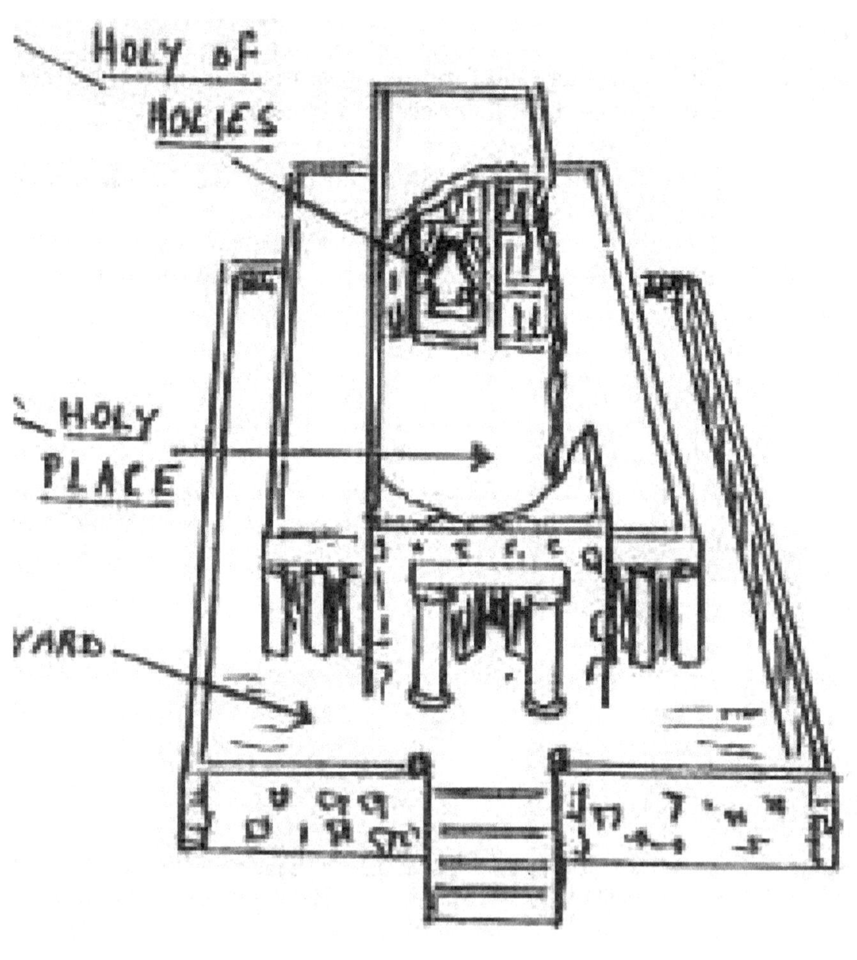

Holy of Holies

HOLY

Meaning: **God is holy. People and things are holy in their relation to God.** **SEE SACRED p 233**

Examples: God called Moses at the burning bush in the desert.
*Then God said, 'Come no closer! Remove the sandals from your feet, for the place on which you are standing is **holy ground**.'*
[Exodus chapter 3 verse 5.]

***Holy, holy, holy** is the LORD of hosts.* [Isaiah chapter 6 verse 3.]

Jesus was teaching in the synagogue.
*Just then there was in their synagogue a man with an unclean spirit, and he cried out, 'What have you to do with us, Jesus of Nazareth? Have you come to destroy us? I know who you are, the **Holy One** of God.'*
[Mark chapter 1 verses 23–24.]

Anna was a **holy woman** who prayed a lot in the temple and followed God's law. She was a prophet who told the people about Jesus.
[Luke chapter 2 verse 38]

Is there a word for **holy** in your language? ....

Talk about some **holy** places or people or things that you know about.

HOLY OF HOLIES

Meaning: **The most special holy place in the Jewish temple where the tabernacle was kept. Only the Chief Priest was allowed to go there once each year.**

Examples: Moses told the workers: *Make a curtain to separate the holy place from the **most holy place** ... Inside the **most holy place**, you must put the sacred chest that has the place of mercy on its lid.*
[Exodus chapter 26 verse 31, 34.]

*Behind the curtain was the **most holy** place. Only the high priest could go into the (**most holy part**) of the tent. And he went in only once a year.* [Hebrews chapter 9 verses 3, 7.]

Is there a word in your language for a place where only a special person can go?...............

Talk about special holy places that you know about.

Holy Spirit

HOLY SPIRIT

Meaning: **The Holy Spirit is the Spirit of God—the giver of life to all creation.**

Jesus sent the Holy Spirit as a gift to his followers after his life, death and resurrection.

Christians believe the Holy Spirit is the third Person of the Holy Trinity.

SEE TRINITY p 269

(A Person in the Holy Trinity is not like a human person.)

Note: Christians also have other names for the Holy Spirit. For example: *Spirit of God; Paraclete; Advocate (John chapter 14 verses 16, 26); Spirit of Truth* (John chapter 14 verses 17, 26).

Examples: *In the beginning, before the world was created, the* ***Spirit of God*** *rested over the waters.* [Genesis chapter 1 verse 2.]

... when Jesus had been baptised, just as he came up from the water, suddenly the heavens were opened to him and he saw the ***Spirit of God*** *descending like a dove and alighting on him.*
[Matthew chapter 3 verse 16.]

Jesus promised his disciples that after his death, God would send the **Holy Spirit** to teach them and remind them of all he had told them.
[John chapter 14 verse 26]

What do you call the **Holy Spirit** in your language? ....

Talk about how the **Holy Spirit** has made a difference in your life or in the lives of others you know.

When Jesus rode into Jerusalem the people shouted '<u>Hosanna</u>'

HOPE

Meaning: **Expecting that good things will come from God. Confidence in the future, based upon the resurrection of Jesus.**

Examples: The students came to *Nungalinya* with a lot of **hope** that they would learn important things for their lives.

Happy are those whose help is the God of Jacob, whose ***hope*** *is in the* LORD *their God.* [Psalm 146 verse 5.]

… God chose to make known how great among the Gentiles are the riches of the glory of this mystery, which is Christ in you, the ***hope*** *of glory.* [Colossians chapter 1 verse 27.]

Blessed be the God and Father of our Lord Jesus Christ! By God's great mercy, God has given us a new birth into a living ***hope*** *through the resurrection of Jesus Christ from the dead …* [1 Peter chapter 1 verse 3.]

What is the word for **hope** in your language?..

Talk about some of your **hopes** for the future.

HOSANNA

Meaning: **Hosanna comes from a Hebrew word that means 'please save us'. It comes from Psalm 118 verse 25. The Israelites used to sing this psalm from the bible on one of their holy days.**

Example: When Jesus rode into Jerusalem on the donkey before he was crucified, all the people shouted out to him, **'Hosanna!'**
[John chapter 12 verse12–14.]

What do you do and say when people visit your community?.................................

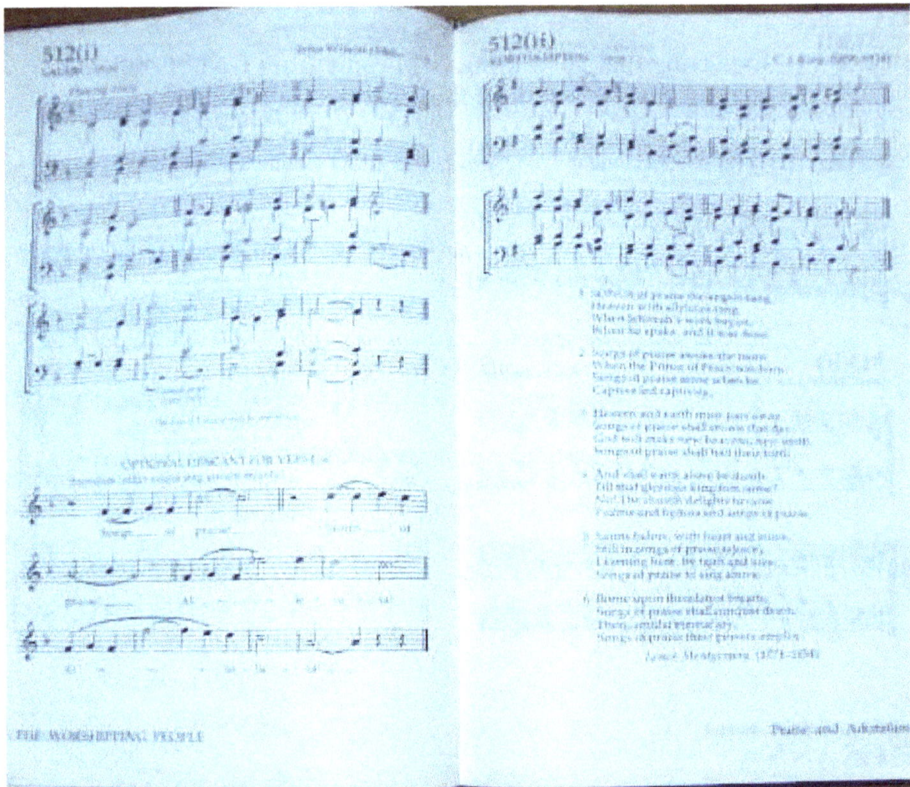

Hymn

HUMILITY

Meaning: **Not being boastful. Not thinking you are more important than other people, but being humble.**

Example: I (Paul) ask you to lead a life worthy of your Christian vocation. You must always have **humility** and be gentle and patient, too, in bearing with one another's faults. [Ephesians chapter 4 verse 2.]

The soldier said he wasn't important enough for Jesus to come to his house to cure his servant. The soldier showed great **humility**. [Matthew chapter 8 verses 6–8.]

What is the word for **humility** in your language?...

Talk about what true humility means.

HYMN

Meaning: **A song of praise to God. The Israelites and Jesus and his followers sang psalms. Psalms are like hymns for us. We sing hymns in church.**

Example: On the evening before he was crucified, Jesus and his disciples ate the last supper. *When they had sung the* ***hymn****, they went out to the Mount of Olives.* [Mark chapter 14 verse 26.]

Is there a word for **hymn** in your language? ....

Talk about some of your favourite **hymns**.

An idol worshipped like a god

I

IDOL

Meaning: **A thing such as a stone, tree, picture, or statue that people worshipped like a god.**

Examples: The Israelites wanted to worship the **idol (the gold calf)** which Aaron made out of their golden rings. [Exodus chapter 32 verses 1–6]

The Second Commandment says we must not worship **idols.**

Is there a word like **idol** in your language?...

Talk about what an **idol** might be in your community.

IMAGE

Meanings: 1 **We are made in the image of God.**

2 **A photo, a painting, a statue which reminds us of someone we love—such as a family member, a famous or holy person, even Jesus or his mother. But we do not worship the picture or statue.**

Example: *So God created humankind ... God created them in the **image** of God; male and female God created them.* [Genesis chapter 1 verse 27.]

*Jesus is the **image** of the invisible God, the firstborn of all creation.* [Colossians chapter 1 verse 15.]

Is there a word like **image** (photograph, painting, statue) in your language?.......................

Talk about some **images** (paintings, photographs) that are special for you.

Incarnation

IMMORTAL

Meaning: **Immortal means living forever.**
When we are raised up by Jesus we will never die again.

Examples: *... this * mortal body must put on* ***immortality.***
[1 Corinthians chapter 15 verse 53.]

Christians believe that the human soul is **immortal.**

God is **immortal.**

Is there a word like **immortal** in your language?..

Does your culture have an idea of living forever?

* A mortal body will die.

INCARNATION

Meaning: **The name of the most important Christian teaching—that the Word of God has become flesh.**
God has taken an earthly bodily form in Jesus Christ so that we might be taken into the life of God.

Examples: *And the Word became flesh and lived among us ...*
[John chapter 1 verse 14.]

Is there an idea anything like **incarnation** in your culture and your stories?.....................

Sweet smelling <u>incense</u>
was burnt on the altar

INCENSE

Meaning: **The sweet smell of some kinds of wood or tree gum when it is burnt.**

Incense was often used in long ago times during religious ceremonies. In some churches it is still used sometimes today.

The smoke of incense going up can be a sign of our prayers going to God.

Examples: When the Israelites were ready to worship God in the sacred tent, 'the gold incense altar was set up in front of the curtain, and sweet-smelling **incense** was burnt on it'. [Exodus chapter 40 verse 26.]

According to the custom of the priests, Zechariah had been chosen to go into the Lord's temple that day to burn **incense,** while the people stood outside praying. [Luke chapter 1 verses 9–10.]

Do you have anything like **incense** in your community customs?.........................

Does your church use **incense**? Talk about times when your church uses **incense**.

ISRAEL

Meaning: **In the Bible, Israel is the name of the nation made up of the 12 tribes who came from Jacob.**

Jacob's other name was 'Israel', so his children and grandchildren were called Israelites.

Israel is also the name of the modern state of the Israeli people.

SEE ISRAELITES p 129 HEBREWS p 111

Example: *The days are surely coming says the LORD, when I will make a new covenant with the house of* ***Israel.*** [Jeremiah chapter 31 verse 31.]

What is the difference between tribe and clan in your community?

Look up the bible and find the names of the 12 tribes of Israel.
[Genesis chapter 49 verses 1–28.]

The people who come from Jacob's Tribe are <u>Israelites</u>

ISRAELITES

Meaning: **Israel-ites are the people in the Bible who come from Jacob's tribe.**

This word comes from 'Israel' (Jacob's other name) which means: 'one who is strong with God'. [Genesis chapter 32 verse 28.]

Sometimes the Israelites are also called Hebrews or Jews.

Examples: *Then the LORD spoke to Moses, 'Go and tell Pharaoh king of Egypt to let the* ***Israelites*** *go out of his land.'* [Exodus chapter 6 verse 13.]

The **Israelites** wandered for many years in the desert.

Does your language have special names for different clans and tribes? Write some of them here. ....

What is the name of your tribe or clan? ....

Jesus

J

JERUSALEM

Meaning: **The holy city of the Jewish people in Palestine. It was the most important city in the time of Jesus, and he often visited it. The city of Jerusalem is still there today.**

Examples: Jesus rode into **Jerusalem** on a donkey. All the people took palm branches and went out to meet him. [John chapter 12 verses 12–15.]

When [Saul] had come to **Jerusalem**, he tried to join the disciples and they were all afraid of him, for they did not believe that he was a disciple. [Acts of the Apostles chapter 9 verse 26.]

What is the name of an important city near your home?......................................

Find a map or a picture of **Jerusalem.** Talk about what the city looks like now.

JESUS

Meaning: **A name often used for Jewish boys and men long ago. Joshua is the Hebrew word for Jesus and it means 'Yahweh/Yahu is salvation'.**

SEE JESUS CHRIST p 131

Talk about some names often used for boys and men in your community. What are some names often used for girls and women?

Jesus Christ

JESUS CHRIST

Meaning: **Jesus of Nazareth, part of the family of Mary and Joseph, lived, taught, died on a cross in Galilee and rose from the dead two thousand years ago. The four gospels are written about him.**

'Christ' means 'the one anointed with the Spirit'. The Jews who followed Jesus believed he was the Messiah promised by God from a long time ago.

Christians believe that Jesus Christ, one person, is fully human and fully God. He is "God with us", the presence of the second person of the Holy Trinity in our midst. [Matthew chapter 1 verse 23.]

SEE JESUS p 131 CHRIST p 45 ANOINT p 11 TRINITY p 269

Examples: At first, the disciples called him Jesus. But when they realised he was the Messiah sent by God, they began to call him **Jesus Christ.**

Jesus said to his disciples, But who do you say I am?
Simon Peter answered, 'You are the **Christ,** the Son of the living God.'
[Matthew chapter 16 verses 15–16.]

What is the word for **Jesus Christ** in your language? ....

Talk about what Aboriginal Australians say about **Jesus Christ**?

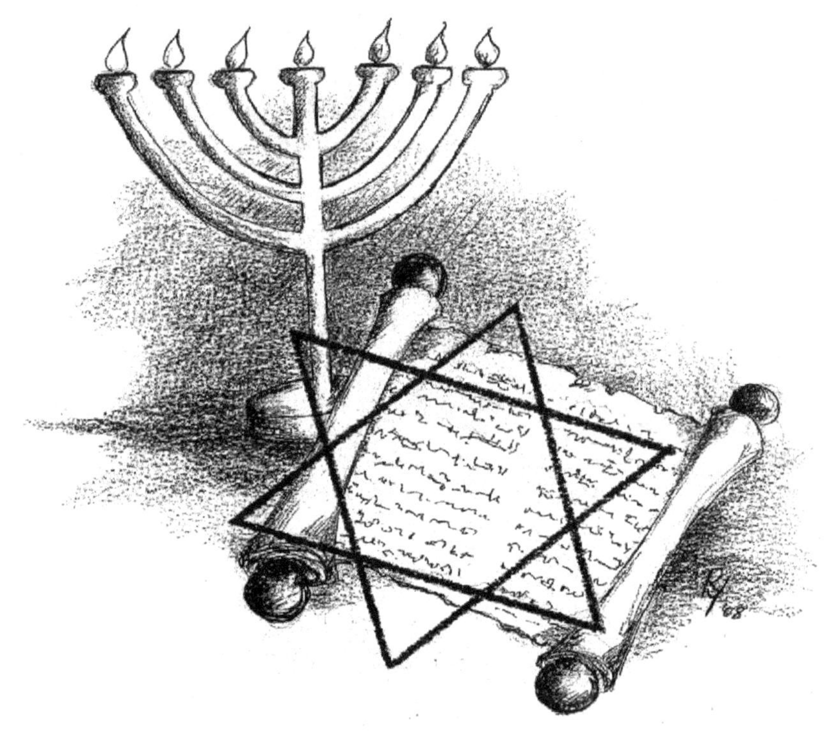

Symbols of Judaism

JUBILEE

Meaning: **Jubilee is a Hebrew word that means 'trumpet'. In Old Testament times, Israelites blew the trumpet at the beginning of the jubilee year. The jubilee year happened every 7 years. There was a special jubilee every 50 years (the year after 7 x 7 = 49 years).**

In the Jubilee year, the Israelites had to free the slaves, give back land, and wipe out any debts that people had.

Example: 'Count 7 times 7 years, a total of 49 years. Then on the 10th day of the 7th month, the Day of Atonement, send someone to blow a trumpet throughout the whole land. In this way you shall set the 50th year apart and proclaim freedom to all the inhabitants of the land.' [Lev. 25:8–10.]

Does your community have special years of celebration like a **jubilee year**?................

Talk about what you do at these times.

JUDAISM or JEWISH RELIGION

Meaning: **The name of the religion, customs and culture of the Jewish people, from long ago up to now.**

Judaism comes from the customs and laws given to Jewish (Israelite) people through Moses and the Prophets long ago. Judaism developed gradually after the time of the Babylonian exile.

These customs and laws are written in the books of the Old Testament part of the Bible.

Examples: The most important place for **Judaism** is Jerusalem.

The religion of the family of Jesus was **Judaism**.

Judaism is still the religion of the Jewish people.

Have you met any **Jewish** people?

Judge
(Deborah)

JUDGES

Meaning: **These were wise tribal elders who were leaders of the Israelites before they had a king.**

Some of the famous judges were Deborah, Gideon and Samson.

Example: The Book of **Judges** in the Bible tells the story of how the Judges, with God's help, led the Israelites to freedom from enemies.

Is there a special word for leaders or elders in your culture? ....

Talk about some elders or peacemakers that you know.

JUDGMENT or JUDGE

Meaning: **God judges us for what we have done in life.**

Examples: On the day of **judgment,** God will separate the good people from the bad people. [Matthew chapter 25 verse 31 and following]

And I saw the dead, great and small, standing before the throne. And books were opened. Also another book was opened, the book of life.
And the dead were ***judged*** by what those books said they had done.
[Revelations chapter 20 verse 12.]

Jesus said: *Do not* ***judge****, so that you may not be* ***judged.*** *For with the* ***judgment*** *you make you will be* ***judged,*** *and the measure you give will be the measure you get.* [Matthew chapter 7 verses 1–2.]

Is there a word for **judgment** in your language?..

Talk about what you think Jesus meant in Matthew chapter 25 verses 31–46

Justice

JUSTICE

Meaning: **The right way to behave towards God, yourself and other people. It means being fair to other people.**

Example: Through the prophets, God kept on telling the Hebrews to be fair to everybody, especially poor people. [Exodus chapter 22 verses 21–22.]

Jesus told the Pharisees: You give gifts to the temple but you forget *about **justice** and the love of God.* [Luke chapter 11 verse 42.]

What is the word for **justice** in your language?..

Talk about what happens when there is no **justice**.

JUSTIFICATION

Meaning: **The gift of forgiveness and friendship God gives to us through Jesus Christ.**

Examples: *... all have sinned and fall short of the glory of God; they are now **justified** by [God's] grace as a gift, through the redemption that is in Christ Jesus.* [Romans chapter 3 verses 23–24.]

Justification is God's gift to us. Jesus *was handed over to death for our trespasses and was raised for our **justification**.* [Romans chapter 4 verse 25.]

*Since we are **justified** by faith, we have peace with God through our Lord Jesus Christ.* [Romans chapter 5 verse 1.]

Holy Spirit help
us in our Life
Peace
Hope
Life
GOOD NEWS BIBLE
Live right
Obey God's words
Forgiveness
Love
Pray for
eachother
Help oneanother

Justify

JUSTIFY

Meaning: **To make a person right with others.**
To make us right with God.

Examples: There was a lawyer who asked Jesus a tricky question about eternal life. Jesus told him he must love his neighbour. But the lawyer wanted to **justify** himself and asked, Who is my neighbour? [Luke chapter 10 verse 29.]

A lot of bad things happened to Job. Job complained to God that it was not fair because he had done nothing wrong, he was a very good person. Job tried to **justify** himself rather than God. [Job chapter 32 verse 2.]

King

K

KING

Meaning: **The leader or ruler of Israel at one time in history.**

Examples: The elders of Israel came to the prophet Samuel and said, 'Give us a **king** to be the boss over us, like the other nations.' [1 Samuel chapter 8 verse 6.]

Saul was made the first **King** of Israel.

Does your language have a word for **king**?..

KINGDOM OF GOD or KINGDOM OF HEAVEN

Meaning: **God's kingdom is wherever God is loved and where God's laws are obeyed.**

Jesus taught that God was coming to God's people to bring healing, justice and peace. He called this God's Kingdom. It was beginning already with Jesus.

We are called to be part of God's Kingdom by the way we live and act.

Example: The Pharisees asked Jesus when the **kingdom of God** was coming.
*Jesus said: The **kingdom of God** is among you.*
[Luke chapter 17 verses 20–21.]

Jesus said: *'The time is fulfilled, and the **kingdom of God** has come near; repent and believe in the good news.'* [Mark chapter 1 verse 15.]

Read more stories about what **God's Kingdom** is like in Matthew chapter 13 verses 44 and verses 47–50.

Talk about **God's Kingdom** or **Heaven** in your language.

Lamb

L

LAMB

Meaning: **A baby sheep or a young sheep, not more than 1 year old.**

SEE LAMB OF GOD p 145 PASSOVER p 193

Examples: Many people like to cook and eat roast **lamb.** At barbecues, they like to cook **lamb** chops.

In Old Testament times, Moses taught the people to offer 2 **lambs** to God every day – one in the morning and one in the evening:
*Now this is what you shall offer on the altar: two **lambs** a year old regularly each day.* [Exodus chapter 29 verse 38.]

What are the words for sheep and **lamb** in your language?..

Have you ever seen a **lamb**? Talk about what they look like.

LAMB OF GOD

Meaning: **Early Christians began to call Jesus 'Lamb of God' because he offered himself to God on the cross at the time of Passover.**

SEE PASSOVER LAMB p 193

Examples: When John the Baptist saw Jesus coming towards him, he said,
*Here is the **Lamb of God** who takes away the sins of the world!* [John chapter 1 verse 29.]

John saw a vision. 'Then I saw standing between the throne with its four animals and the circle of the elders, **a Lamb** that seemed to have been sacrificed. [Revelation chapter 5 verse 6.]

In some Church services, Christians pray and sing to Jesus as the **Lamb of God.** Does this happen in your Church? Talk about what those prayers are.

Lamp

LAMENT

Meaning: **To feel sorry about something. A sad song or sad story about something. In the Bible, the book of Lamentations tells about sad parts of Israel's history.**

Examples: People **lament** when they hear about someone dying.

In the books of the Old Testament, there are many **laments** about sad things. For example, when Abner was killed, King David was very sad. He wept aloud at Abner's grave and made up a **lament** for him.
[2 Samuel chapter 3 verse 33–34.]

Jesus wept about what would happen to Jerusalem. He **lamented** the destruction that would happen. [Matthew chapter 23 verses 37–39.]

What is the word for **lament** in your language?..

Talk about some of the sad songs about sad things in your community stories.

LAMP or LAMPSTAND

Meaning 1: **Something used to give light when it is dark.**
In Old Testament times, people burned a wick soaked in oil to give light. Now we have electric power to give light.

A lampstand is what you put the lamp on to make it high.

Examples 1: King Solomon built a very big Temple. In it there were ten **lampstands** made of gold. [1 Kings chapter 7, verses 48–50.]

In John's vision of the New Jerusalem: *there will be no more night; they need no light of* ***lamp*** *or sun, for the Lord God will be their light* … [Revelations chapter 22 verse 5.]

Meaning 2: **Lamp can also be a sign for light in the mind.**

Examples 2: *Your word is a* ***lamp*** *to my feet and a light to my path.* [Psalm 119 verse 105.]
You will do well to be attentive to this (prophetic message) as to a ***lamp*** *shining in a dark place* … [1 Peter chapter 1 verse 19.]

What other things can you use for light if there is no electricity?..............................

In traditional communities, before electricity, what did your community use for light at night?

Last Supper

LAST SUPPER

Meaning: **The meal that Jesus had with his followers on the night before he was crucified.**

This is the beginning of the Christian ceremony of the Eucharist or Holy Communion, because Jesus said, 'Do this in memory of me.' **[Luke chapter 22 verses 19–20.]**

SEE LORD'S SUPPER p 159 EUCHARIST p 77 HOLY COMMUNION p 51 PASSOVER p 193

Example: Every year on Thursday in the week before Easter (Holy Week), Christians have church services to remember the **Last Supper**.

Do any of your ceremonies have an important meal as part of them?

Talk about what happens at these meals.

LAW

Meaning: **Rules and customs that tell people how to behave and how to live their lives.**

In the Bible, the law means the rules for living a good life and for worshipping God in the right way. God gave this law to the people through Moses.

Jesus said the most important commandments of the law were to love God and to love our neighbour.

SEE PENTATEUCH p 197 TORAH p 265

Examples: Jesus said: *"You shall love the lord your God with all your heart, and with all your soul, and with all your mind. This is the greatest and the first commandment. And the second is like it: You shall love your neighbour as yourself. On these two commandments hang all the **law** and the prophets.* [Matthew chapter 22 verses 37–39.]

God gave the Israelites many **laws**. You can read about some of these in the Book of Exodus, chapters 20, 21, 22 and 23.

What is the word for **law** in your language?..

Talk about the meaning of **law and custom** in your communities.

Lent

LENT

Meaning: **The six-week season of the Church year (Liturgical Year) before Easter.**

During Lent, Christians get ready to remember Jesus' death and resurrection at Easter. This often includes more time for prayer, fasting from some food and doing more kind things for other people.

SEE LITURGICAL YEAR p 157

Example: **Lent** begins on Ash Wednesday and it finishes on Holy Saturday, the day before Easter Sunday.

Talk about what you do during **Lent** to get ready for Easter.

LEPER (LEPROSY)

Meaning: **A person with a sickness of the skin called leprosy. People thought they could easily catch the sickness from one another. So lepers had to stay outside the town, away from everybody. [Leviticus chapter 13 verses 47–52.]**

Examples: *A **leper** came to [Jesus] and pleaded on his knees: 'If you want to' he said 'you can cure me.'* [Mark chapter 1 verse 40.]

Jesus went to have dinner at the house of Simon who was a **leper**. [Mark chapter 14 verse 3.]

Today, doctors use medicine to make people with **leprosy** better.

What is the word for **leper** in your language?..

Have you ever seen or heard about anyone who was a **leper**?

Levites

LEVITES

Meaning: **Levites were members of the tribe of Levi. Levi was one of the 12 sons of Jacob (Israel). Israelite priests came from the tribe of Levi.**

Examples: *The **Levites** have no portion [of the land shared out] among you, for the priesthood of the Lord is their heritage;* [Joshua chapter 18 verse7.]

In the New Testament story of the Good Samaritan, we read: *So likewise a **Levite,** when he came to the place and saw him, passed by on the other side.* [Luke chapter 10 verse 32.]

LIBERATOR

Meaning: **A person who frees us from something bad.**
Jesus is our liberator and sets us free.
Jesus frees us so that we can love God and our sisters and brothers.

SEE DELIVERANCE p 69 FREEDOM p 89

Example: At the time of Jesus, the Romans were bosses over the Jewish people. The Jews wanted someone to come as a **liberator** for them, to free them from the Romans.
But Jesus came to be a different kind of **liberator**—he taught them how to be free from all the bad things in their lives.

Is there a word like **liberator** in your language? ....

Do you know any people who are like **liberators**?

LIBERTY SEE FREEDOM p 89

Lion

LIFE

Meaning 1: 1 **Life is what makes you able to grow and change and have children. People, plants and animals have life. They can all grow and change. Things without life are dead.**

SEE ETERNAL LIFE p 75

Example 1: At the start of creation, God gave **life** to plants, animals, fish, birds and people. [Genesis chapter 1, verses 1–31.] **Life** ended when they died.

Meaning 2: **In the New Testament, life often means eternal life.**

Examples 2: Jesus said: *Very truly, I tell you, whoever believes has* ***eternal life.*** [John chapter 6 verse 47.]

Jesus said: *I am the* ***bread of life*** *... the one who eats this bread will live forever.* [John chapter 6 verses 48, 58.]

What is the word for **life** in your language?...

Talk about the **life** God gives us.

LION

Meaning: 1 **A big cat that can kill other animals and people.**

2 **The Bible sometimes uses a lion as a picture for Satan or the devil.**

Example: *Be calm [but look out], because your enemy the devil is prowling round like a roaring* ***lion****, looking for someone to eat.* [1 Peter chapter 5 verse 8.]

There are no **lions** in the Australian bush, but some **lions** now live in zoos in the big cities. Have you ever seen a **lion**? Talk about what they look like.

Lion of the Tribe of Judah

LION OF THE TRIBE OF JUDAH

Meaning: **'Lion of Judah' is sometimes a name for Jesus Christ because a lion is very strong. Also, Jesus belonged to the tribe of Judah, and Judah was the strongest tribe of Israel.**
[Genesis chapter 49 verses 8–9.]

Example: *I began to weep bitterly because no one was found worthy to open the scroll or to look into it. Then one of the elders said to me, "Do not weep. See, the* ***Lion of the Tribe of Judah****, the Root of David, has conquered, so that he can open the scroll …* [Revelation chapter 5 verses 4–5.]

LITURGY

Meaning: **1 A service or ceremony of public worship when people come together to sing hymns, read scripture and pray.**

2 The ceremony of readings, prayers and actions of the Eucharist or Mass, or Communion service.

SEE RITUAL p 227 CEREMONY p 41

Example: The **Liturgy** is what we do when we worship God in church.

Is there a word for ceremonies in your community?......................................

Talk about the different parts of the **Liturgy** and who does them.

LITURGICAL YEAR (CHURCH YEAR)

Meaning: **The church arrangement of the year into spiritual seasons to remember the important events in the life of Jesus.**

Example: In the season of **Advent,** we remember the coming of Jesus and wait for his coming again.
In the **Christmas** season, we remember the birth of Jesus;
In **Lent** we get ready for the most important season in the church year which is **Easter**.
In the **Easter season**, we remember the Resurrection of Jesus.
At **Pentecost**, after Easter, we remember the coming of the Holy Spirit.

Talk about what you do in your community to celebrate these different church seasons of the year.

M & L Joshua

Love

LORD

Meaning: **A person who is a leader or high boss.**

In the Old Testament, Lord is sometimes the word used for God or Yahweh.
In the New Testament, Jesus Christ is often called Lord.

Example: The disciples in the boat during the storm said to Jesus, ***Lord,*** *wake up! Save us before we drown!* [Matthew chapter 8 verse 23.]

Is there a word of respect like **lord** in your language? ....

Talk about what a high boss does in your community.

LORD'S SUPPER — SEE EUCHARIST p 77 BREAKING OF THE BREAD p 33 LAST SUPPER p 149.

LOVE

Meaning: **Love is when you deeply care about another person or other people, and you want the best life for them.**
Love can also mean you really like a person.

God loves all people.

God is love. **[1 John chapter 4 verse 8.]**

Examples: Mothers and fathers **love** their children.

Jesus said: *This is my commandment, that you* ***love*** *one another as I have* ***loved*** *you. No one has greater* ***love*** *than this, to lay down one's life for one's friends.* [John chapter 15 verses 12–13.]

What is the word for **love** in your language?...

Talk about the way Christians **love** one another.
Talk about what it means to say 'God is **love**'.

Loving Kindness

LOVING-KINDNESS

Meaning: **This is the word we use for God's very great kindness and care for us that will never ever stop.**

SEE COMPASSION p 53

Examples: *Give thanks ... for [God] is good,* ***God's love is everlasting.*** [Psalm 107 verse 1.]

Oh give thanks to the God of gods, for [God's] love endures forever. [Psalm 136 verse 2.]

God ... is gracious and merciful, slow to anger, and abounding in steadfast love. [Joel chapter 2 verse 13.]

Manna

M

MAGIC

Meaning: **A special power to make good and bad things happen to people.**

SEE CURSE p 63

Example: For some time, a man named Simon had lived in the city of Samaria. He practised **magic** and claimed to be somebody great. [Acts of the Apostles chapter 8 verse 9.]

What is the word for **magic** in your language?................................

Talk about what happens when people do **magic** in your community.

MANNA

Meaning: **'Manna' is the Hebrew word for 'What is it?' It is the special food God gave the Israelites when they were hungry in the desert after they left Egypt.**
It probably came from insects and it tasted like honey.

Example: In the morning, there was dew all around the camp. When the dew lifted, there on the ground was food that looked like powder, as fine as frost on the ground. The Israelites said, **What is it?** Moses said, This is the bread Yahweh gives you to eat. [Exodus chapter 16 verses 14–16.]

Mary

MARY

Meaning: **In the gospels, Mary is the name of the woman who was the mother of Jesus and the wife of Joseph.**

There were some other women in the gospels called Mary. One of them was Mary Magdalene.

Examples: **...** The Angel Gabriel was sent by God to a town in Galilee called Nazareth, to a virgin engaged to a man whose name was Joseph. The virgin's name was **Mary**. [Luke chapter 1 verses 26–27.]

When Jesus died on the cross: *Many women were also there, looking on from a distance; they had followed Jesus from Galilee and had provided for him. Among them were* ***Mary Magdalene****, and* ***Mary*** *the mother of James and Joseph ...* [Matthew chapter 27 verses 55–56.]

Are there women called **Mary** in your community?

MEDIATOR

Meaning: **A person in the middle of two people or two groups who makes peace or agreement between them.**

Examples: Moses was a **mediator** between God and the Israelites. He stood there praying to God for the people with arms outstretched.
[Exodus chapter 32 verses 30–34]

For there is one God; there is also one ***mediator*** *between God and humankind, Christ Jesus, himself human ...*
[1 Timothy chapter 2 verse 5.]

Is there a word for **mediator** in your language? ....

Do you know someone who is a **mediator**? Talk about what they do.

Memorial

MEMORIAL

Meaning: **Something to help us think about something that happened in the past.**

The Eucharist is a memorial that not only remembers Jesus but makes him present.

A memorial could be a headstone on a grave or a day like Anzac day.

Example: Jacob had a dream one night when God promised to keep him safe wherever he went. When Jacob woke up he said, This place is the house of God. So he took the stone he had slept on and put it there as a **memorial**. [Genesis chapter 28 verses 10–19.]

What are the words in your language for places or ceremonies that remind you of important things in the past?..

Talk about some **memorials** you have in your community.

MERCY

Meaning: **To show kindness to anyone who is suffering, or to someone who has done something wrong to us.**

SEE COMPASSION p 53

Examples: In the Bible, we read about the **mercy** of God, who forgives us and cares for us.

We see the kindness or **mercy** of God when Jesus Christ teaches, heals and cares for the people. [Luke chapter 5 verses 12–13.]

The ten lepers called out to Jesus, saying: *Jesus, Master, have **mercy** on us.* [Luke chapter 17 verse 13.]

Is there a word for **mercy** in your language? ....

Talk about times when someone has given kindness or **mercy** towards you. How did you feel?

Minister

MESSIAH

Meaning: **A special person anointed by God who would come to save the Jews. The Jews looked forward for a long time to the coming of this person, who was called 'messiah'.**

When Jesus came, many people asked him if he was the Messiah, sent by God.

SEE CHOSEN p 43 CHRIST p 45

Examples: The people asked John the Baptist if he was the **messiah.** He said, no, he was not. The **messiah** would come after him. [Luke chapter 3 verse 15.]

Early next morning, Andrew met his brother and said to him, 'We have found the **Messiah'**—which means the Christ—and he took Simon to Jesus. [John chapter 1 verse 41.]

Talk about what you would say in your language to help people understand what **messiah** means.

MINISTER (and MINISTRIES)

Meaning: **A person who works for God as part of the church to help people. The work is called their ministry. There are many different kinds of ministries in the church. Some churches call their ministers 'priests' or 'pastors'.**

Examples: There are many **ministries** in the church: God chose some people to be apostles and prophets and teachers for the church, and some to work miracles or heal the sick or help others.
[1 Corinthians chapter 12 verse 28.]

Barnabas and Saul arrived at Salamis and began to preach God's message ... They had John Mark as a helper. [Acts chapter 13 verse 5.]

St. Paul wrote: *At present, however, I am going to Jerusalem in a* ***ministry*** *to the saints ...* [Romans chapter 15 verse 25.]

Who are some of the **ministers** in your church?...

Talk about the different **ministries** they do.

Moderator

MIRACLE

Meaning: **When something very good happens, even when we think it is impossible, and we do not know how it happened, we say it is a miracle.**

In the Bible, when miracles happened, people believed that God did it.

In the New Testament, miracles are a sign that the Kingdom of God is coming.

Examples: It was a **miracle** when the Israelites got away from the Egyptians by walking through the Red Sea on dry ground. They believed that God made it happen for them. [Exodus chapter 14 verses 21–26.]

When Jesus turned the water into wine at the wedding at Cana, it was a **miracle.** This was a sign of God's power and love for the people. [John chapter 2 verses 1–11.]

Is there a word for **miracle** in your language?..

Talk about some more **miracles** in the Bible. [For example: Matthew chapter 8 verses 1-3; Matthew chapter 14 verses 15–21.]

MODERATOR

Meaning: **The moderator is a man or woman (ordained or lay) who is elected by the members of the synod. The moderator's responsibility is to have the pastoral and administrative oversight of all the churches that belong to the synod. Uniting Churches have a moderator in each synod.**

SEE BISHOP p 27 SYNOD p 255

Example: The members of the synod were meeting to elect a new **Moderator.**

Who is the **Moderator** of your Synod?...

Myrrh

MONEY CHANGER

Meaning: **A person whose job it is to change money from one country to the money of another country.**

In the Bible, when people from another country came to pay the tax at the Jerusalem Temple, they had to change their money into local money.

Example: A **money changer** changes Australian money into the same amount in Chinese money—or some other country's money.

Jesus got angry with the **money changers** and everyone selling things in the temple. He turned over their tables and chased them outside. He said the temple was a place to pray in. [Matthew chapter 21 verses 12–13.]

MYRRH

Meaning: **A perfume that came from a plant in Arabia. It cost a lot of money. Myrrh was one of the gifts that the wise men brought to Jesus when he was born.**

SEE FRANKINCENSE p 89

Example: The three wise men went to see Jesus when he was born.
On entering the house, they saw the child with Mary his mother; and they knelt down and [worshipped him]. Then opening their treasure chests, they offered him gifts of gold, frankincense and ***myrrh.***
[Matthew chapter 2 verse 11.]

What are some sweet-smelling trees that you know about?.................................

MYTH

Meaning: **A myth is like a story that tries to explain important things. The myth helps us to understand them better. Myth is a story-telling way of doing philosophy and theology.**

Example: The story in the Book of Genesis about Adam and Eve and the serpent is a **myth.** [Genesis chapter 2 verses 4–24; chapter 3 verses 1–24.]

Is there a word or an idea like **myth** in your language?...

Talks about some **myths** in your community.

Name

N

NAME

Meaning: **What we call a person or a thing—Mary, tree, chair. In the Bible, there are different names for the One God, for example, Elohim, Adonai (Lord). Yahweh is God's special name.**

In the Bible, names often tell us something important about a person or place. Jacob's new name was Israel. He got this name after he fought with a messenger from God. [Genesis chapter 32 verses 24–28.] Israel means 'one who is strong with God'.

Jacob (Israel) called that place Peniel (Penuel), which means, 'face of God'.

Example: When Elizabeth gave birth to her son, all her relatives and neighbours were happy. They thought the boy's **name** would be Zechariah after his father. *But his mother said, "No, he is to be called John."*
[Luke chapter 1 verses 58–60.]

Does your **name** have a special meaning?...

How many different **names** do you have? (What do people call you?)

Talk about some **names** of people or places that have special meanings.

Nazirite

NATIONS

Meaning: **In the Bible, the nation of Israel had 12 tribes who spoke the same language. There were other nations in the lands around Israel. One of these other nations was Egypt. Another one was Syria. Australia is a nation.**

Examples: God sent Israel a leader who rescued them from the **Syrians.** [2 Kings chapter 13 verse 5.]

Joseph's brothers sold him into slavery in **Egypt.** [Genesis chapter 37 verses 12–36.]

In the Book of Exodus we can read about how the Israelites got away from slavery in **Egypt.**

Is there a word like **nation** in your language?..

Talk about some **nations** today that you know about.

NAZIRITE

Meaning: **In Old Testament times, a Nazirite was someone who wanted to live a very good life. They made a promise that they would let their hair grow long, and they would not drink alcohol or touch a dead body. Sometimes parents made this promise for their child. [1 Samuel chapter 1 verses 10–11.]**

Examples: Manoah's wife could not have children.
And the angel of the LORD appeared to the woman and said to her, "Although you are barren, having borne no children, you shall conceive and bear a son. Now be careful not to drink wine or strong drink, or to eat anything unclean, for you shall conceive and bear a son. No razor is to come on his head, for the boy shall be a ***nazirite*** *to God from birth.*
... The woman bore a son, and named him Samson. [Judges chapter 13 verses 2–5, verse 24.]

Hannah, wife of Elkanah, could not have children. She was sad. She went to the temple and prayed: *Oh Lord of hosts if only you will ... remember me, and not forget your servant, but will give to your servant a male child, then I will set him before you as a* ***nazirite*** *until the day of his death. He shall drink neither wine nor intoxicants and no razor shall touch his head.*
... In due time, Hannah conceived and bore a son. She named him Samuel. [First Samuel chapter 1, verses 11, 20.]

Is there a word or an idea like **nazirite** in your language or community?..........................

New Covenant

NEW COVENANT

Meaning: **In the Old Testament, the Covenant was the agreement God made with the Israelites: that God would be their God and would look after them, and they would be God's people.**
[Genesis chapter 9 verse 9; Genesis chapter 15 verse 18; Exodus chapter 2 verse 24.]

The New Covenant is the agreement and promise God made to all people in the life and death of Jesus Christ.

SEE COVENANT p 59

Examples: *The days are surely coming, says the Lord, when I will make a* ***new covenant*** *with the house of Israel … It will not be like the covenant that I made with their ancestors …*
But this is the covenant that I will make with the house of Israel after those days … :I will put my law within them, and I will write it on their hearts; and I will be their God and they shall be my people.
[Jeremiah chapter 31 verses 31–33.]

At the last supper, Jesus shared bread and wine with his disciples.
He shared the bread. *And he did the same with the cup after supper, saying, 'This cup that is poured out for you is the* ***new covenant*** *in my blood … '*
[Luke chapter 22 verse 20.]

Oath

O

OATH

Meaning: **In Old Testament times, people called on God's name to show they would tell the truth. This was called making an oath.**

Example: *You have learnt how it was said to our ancestors: You must not break your **oath**, but must fulfil your **oaths** to the Lord.*
[Matthew chapter 5 verses 33.]

Have you ever heard anyone make an **oath**?.......................................

OBEDIENCE

Meaning: **To hear in our ears and our heart what God wants us to do, and then to do those things God wants us to do.**

To do what people in charge tell us to do, as long as they are good things.

Examples: God gave Moses and the Israelites the Ten Commandments and told them how to live. All the people promised their **obedience** to God: They promised to do all the things that Yahweh wanted them to do.
[Exodus chapter 20 verses 1–21; Exodus chapter 24 verse 3.]

What is the word for **obedience** in your language?..

Talk about the good things that happen when people show **obedience** to God and to the people in charge.

Offering

OFFERING

Meaning: **In the Old Testament, the Israelites often gave animals, bread and oil as gifts for God. The gift was called an offering. They put the offerings on the altar. The animal was killed and burnt. Its blood was poured out on the altar.**

They did this to say 'sorry' to God, or to please God, or to make peace with one another.

[See Exodus chapter 29; Leviticus Chapters 6 and 7.]

Some Christians see the Eucharist as our participation in the one offering and sacrifice when Jesus gave his life on the cross.

Giving money and other things to the church for God's work is called an offering.

SEE BURNT OFFERING p 35

Examples: In church ceremonies today, we make an **offering** of our lives to God.
St. Paul encourages the people to offer themselves to God:
*Think of God's mercy, my sisters and brothers, and worship [God] in a way that is worthy of thinking beings, by **offering** your living bodies as a holy sacrifice, truly pleasing to God.* [Romans chapter 12 verse 1.]

Paul told them he was going to Jerusalem to help the people. 'For the churches in Macedonia and Achaia have freely decided to give an **offering** to help the poor among God's people in Jerusalem. [Romans chapter 15 verse 25–26.]

What is the word for **offering** in your language?..

Talk about what kind of **offerings** you give in your church community.

Oil

OIL

Meaning: **Oil in the Bible is the juice of the small berry fruit that grows on the olive tree. Olive trees grow very easily in the land of the Israelites. In Old Testament times, oil was used in Jewish religious ceremonies to anoint kings or priests.**

Oil was used a lot for food and cooking.

In the New Testament, oil is used to anoint sick people.

Some churches anoint with oil at the time of baptism, confirmation and ordination.

SEE ANOINT p 11

Examples: *The Lord said to Moses: ... Dress Aaron in the priestly clothes, then use the sacred olive* ***oil*** *to ordain him and dedicate him to me as my priest.*
[Exodus chapter 40 verse 13.]

David is anointed as king: *The Lord said, 'Rise and anoint him for this is the one.' Then Samuel took the horn of* ***oil,*** *and anointed him ...*
[1 Samuel chapter 16 verses 12–13.]

If you are sick, ask the church leaders to come and pray for you. Ask them to put olive ***oil*** *on you in the name of the Lord. If you have faith when you pray for sick people, they will get well.*
[James chapter 5 verses 14–15.]

What is the word for **oil** in your language?..
Where does it come from?...

Have you seen someone anointed with **oil** in your community? Talk about what happened.

Ordination

ORAL

Meaning: **Words from your mouth—instead of written in a book or on paper.**

SEE WRITTEN p 279 PARABLE p 189

Examples: Away back in the beginning, stories of the Dreaming got passed on by the elders to the young people in **oral words.** Then they passed on the stories to their children in **oral words**.

Early Christians did the same as the Aborigines. In the beginning, they passed on the stories about Jesus by **oral words**. After about 70 or 80 years, they began to write the stories in books. Then the **oral stories** became written stories.

Jesus taught the people with many stories. We call them parables. Examples are the story of the lost son, the sower of seed and the Good Samaritan. [Luke chapter 15 verses 11–32; Matthew chapter 13 verses 1–9; Luke chapter 10 verses 25–37.]

Talk about one of your favourite stories that Jesus told.

ORDINATION

Meaning: **This is a church word for the ceremony when a bishop prays for the Holy Spirit to come upon a person, making that person a bishop, priest or deacon.**
In some churches, ordination is when the members of the presbytery together act like a collective bishop, and make someone a minister or a deacon.
That person is ordained.

In the Catholic Church, ordination is called the Sacrament of Holy Orders.

In some churches, the ordinary people or lay people have a say in who is ordained.

Example: **Ordination** only happens after a person has prayed and studied for some years, and after the bishop agrees that they are ready to serve the people in the church.

Talk about some people you know who are **ordained.** Talk about how they serve the church.

Palace

P

PALACE

Meaning: **A palace is a very big house with lots of rooms. It costs a lot of money. Kings and queens live in palaces.**

Example: King Solomon built a **palace** for himself and it took him 13 years. [1 Kings chapter 7 verses 1–9.]

Do you know about any **palaces**? Who lives in them?

PARABLE

Meaning: **A story about ordinary things that Jesus used to teach important things about God and about the coming of the Kingdom of God.**

SEE ORAL p 187

Examples: Jesus often taught his followers through **parables.** For example, there is the Parable of the Good Samaritan, and the Parable of the lost sheep. [See Matthew chapter 13.]

And Jesus told them many things in ***parables****, saying: "Listen! A sower went out to sow.* [Matthew chapter 13 verse 3.]

Do you have anything like **parables** that you teach in your culture?...........................

Talk about some other **parables** in the gospels you know.

Paradise

PARADISE

Meaning: **In the story about Adam and Eve, Paradise is another name for the Garden of Eden where they lived.**
[Genesis chapter 2 verses 8–10.]

People think of paradise as a place of great happiness after death.

SEE HEAVEN p 111

Example: Two thieves who were crucified with Jesus asked him to remember them. Jesus said to them: *Truly I tell you, today you will be with me in* ***paradise.*** [Luke chapter 23 verse 43.]

PARDON SEE FORGIVE p 87

PASSION

Meaning: **A very strong feeling—for example, of love, or sadness or anger.**

In the New Testament, passion means the sufferings and death of Jesus.

The story of the passion is the part of the Gospels that tells about the sufferings and death of Jesus.

Examples: Especially at Easter time on Good Friday, Christians read again the story of the **Passion** of Jesus.

Jesus showed himself to many people after his **Passion**. For forty days after he died, he continued to appear to them and tell them about the Kingdom of God. [Acts of the Apostles chapter 1 verse 3.]

Is there a word or idea like **passion** in your language? ....

Talk about the **passion** of Jesus Christ.

Pastor

PASSOVER

Meaning: **A special Jewish meal every year to remember the Exodus journey, when Moses led the Israelites to freedom from slavery in Egypt. [Exodus chapter 12 verses 1–14.]**

Examples: *On the first day of Unleavened Bread, when the* ***Passover*** *lamb is sacrificed, his disciples said to Jesus, 'Where do you want us to go and make the preparations for you to eat the* ***Passover****?'*
[Mark chapter 14 verse 12.]

On the night before he died on the cross, Jesus had the **Passover** meal (Last Supper) with his disciples. [Luke chapter 22 verses 14–23.]

PASSOVER LAMB

Meaning: **1 The lamb the Israelites had to cook for the Passover meal. They ate it with all their family. [Exodus chapter 12 verses 3–10.]**

2 Jesus ate the last Passover meal with his disciples on the night before he died. Just as the Passover lambs were killed at that time, so Jesus was killed at that time. Because of that, early Christians called Jesus a Passover lamb.

SEE PASSOVER p 193 LAMB OF GOD p 145

Example: Paul told the early Christians to celebrate the feast of Passover by being good because ***our Passover lamb*** *is Christ, who has already been sacrificed.* [1 Corinthians chapter 5 verses 7–8.]

PASTOR

Meaning: **Another name for the priest or minister in a church community. The pastor looks after the spiritual life of the people.**

Example: Some churches call the minister 'father' or 'reverend'. Some other churches call the minister **'pastor'.**

Is there a special word in your language for the person who looks after the spiritual life of the people?..

Find out which churches call their ministers **'pastors'**.

Peace

PATIENCE

Meaning: **Patience helps us to keep going in life and work when things are hard. A patient person does not give up easily.**

Patience is a fruit of the Holy Spirit. It is a gift of God.

Examples: *Rejoice in hope, be* ***patient*** *in suffering, persevere in prayer.* [Romans chapter 12 verse 12.]

Love is ***patient****, love is kind.* [1 Corinthians chapter 13 verse 4.]

The fruit of the Spirit is love, joy, peace, ***patience*** *…* [Galatians chapter 5 verse 22.]

What is the word for **patience** in your language?......................................

Talk about some times when you would like to show more **patience.**

PEACE

Meaning: **When things are quiet and there is no trouble, when there is no fighting.**

Being quiet and happy in your inside self, because you are well in every way.

God gives us peace through Jesus Christ.

Examples: The Israelites believed that **peace** was a gift from God. They used to wish each other **peace** just as we say 'good morning'. The Hebrew word for **peace** is 'shalom'.

When Jesus showed himself to the disciples after his resurrection, he said to them: *'****Peace*** *be with you!'*. [Luke chapter 24 verse 36.]

Therefore, since we are justified by faith, we have ***peace*** *with God through our Lord Jesus Christ.* [Romans chapter 5 verse 1.]

Christian churches often have a **'sign of peace'** in their church services.

What is the word for **peace** in your language?..

Does your church have a **peace greeting** in its services? Talk about how the people do this.

THE OLD TESTAMENT

Pentateuch

PENTATEUCH

Meaning: **A Greek word that means the first 5 books of the Bible: Genesis, Exodus, Leviticus, Numbers and Deuteronomy. Jewish people call these books the Torah. They are also known as the Law of Moses.**

SEE LAW p 149 TORAH p 265

Example: The 5 books of the **Pentateuch** are very important for the Hebrew people. Many of their laws are in the Pentateuch.

What is the word for law in your language?..

PENTECOST

Meaning: **In Old Testament times, this was a holiday when the farmers celebrated the harvest of their crops. It is still a Jewish celebration that happens 50 days after the Passover.**

For Christians, it is 50 days after Easter Sunday when we remember the coming of the Holy Spirit.

SEE LITURGICAL YEAR p 157

Example: *When the day of* ***Pentecost*** *had come, they were all together in one place. And suddenly from heaven there came a sound like the rush of a violent wind, and it filled the entire house where they were sitting.*
[Acts chapter 2 verses 1–2.]

Talk about what your Church does to celebrate **Pentecost** Sunday.

Perfume

PERFECTION

Meaning: **The very best someone or something can be.**
Only God is perfect.
In the New Testament, perfection means to live a fully grown-up Christian life. [1 Corinthians chapter 2 verse 6.]

Example: Jesus told his followers that it was not good enough just to love family and friends and the people who were nice to them. To follow Jesus means loving everyone, just as God loves everyone. Jesus told the people:
*Be **perfect** ... as your heavenly Father is **perfect.***
[Matthew chapter 5 verses 43–48.]

What is the word for **perfection** in your language?..

Talk about what it means to be a **perfect** or fully grown-up Christian.

PERFUME

Meaning: **Something that smells very nice. Some trees or flowers have a sweet perfume. Sometimes perfume is in a liquid or ointment or cream. Another word for perfume is scent.**

SEE FRANKINCENSE p 89 MYRRH p 173

Examples: **Perfumes** were very important in Old Testament times. People used them a lot in everyday life. For example, they burnt spices to make a sweet smell and a lot of white smoke. They anointed people with sweet-smelling perfume.

Six days before the Passover Jesus came to Bethany ... There they gave a dinner for him ... Mary took a pound of costly **perfume** *made of pure nard, anointed Jesus' feet, and wiped them with her hair. The house was filled with the fragrance of the* **perfume**. [John chapter 12 verses 1–3]

After the death of Jesus, Joseph of Arimathaea put the body of Jesus in a cave. Some women came with spices and ointments with a nice **perfume** to put on his body. [Luke chapter 23 verses 55–56.]

What is the word for **perfume** in your language?..

Talk about some trees and flowers that have very nice **perfumes**.
Talk about some ways we use perfumes these days.

Pharisees

PERSECUTION

Meaning: **Making trouble for people and making them suffer for what they believe or who they are. Sometimes it even means killing people for what they believe or who they are.**

Examples: One of the early Christians who suffered **persecution** for believing in Jesus was Stephen. Stephen was killed by stoning because of what he said about Jesus. [Acts chapter 7 verses 55–60.]

For hundred of years, the Jewish people suffered **persecution** from Christians.

In some parts of the world today, Christians still suffer **persecution**. They are often put in jail and killed.

Is there a word like **persecution** in your language?...

Talk about some of the people who suffer **persecution** today.

PHARISEES

Meaning: **A group of Jews who very carefully obeyed every law of Moses. Many of them would have been good people.**

Examples: *Then **Pharisees** and scribes came to Jesus from Jerusalem and said, "Why do your disciples break the tradition of the elders?*
[Matthew chapter 15 verses 1–2]

*You **Pharisees** and teachers of the Law of Moses are in for trouble! You're nothing but show-offs.* [Matthew chapter 23 verse 23.]

Find some more things in Matthew's gospel that Jesus said to the **Pharisees.**

Think about how you would tell people in your communities what kind of a person a **Pharisee** was.

Pillar

PILLAR

Meaning: **A tall piece of stone, like a tree trunk that props up or supports a building.**
When a pillar stands by itself, it is there to remember something.

Example: After God gave Moses the Commandments on Mt. Sinai, Moses built an altar at the bottom of the mountain and put up 12 **standing stones** for the 12 tribes of Israel. These **12 pillars** were there to remind the Israelites of God's commandments and their promise to obey them.
[Exodus chapter 24 verses 4–5.]

Is there a word for a high stone in the bush in your language?......................................

Look up some other chapters in the Bible where people put up **pillars of stone** to remember something special. [For example, Genesis chapter 28 verses 10–19, especially verse 18—Jacob's dream; Genesis chapter 35 verse 20—Rachel's grave.]

PLAGUE

Meaning: **A very bad sickness that a lot of people catch, or a lot of pests making trouble for people.**

Examples: In some countries, AIDS is a **plague.**

Cane toads are becoming a **plague** in northern Australia. Sometimes in Australia there are grasshopper **plagues.**

When the Egyptians would not let the Israelites go, we are told they were punished with the **ten plagues**. [Exodus chapters 7 to 11.]

Have you seen a **plague** of anything in your community? Talk about what happened.

Potter

PLOUGH

Meaning: **A plough is a tool that farmers use to dig up the ground before planting food crops.**

We can use this idea—to dig up or plough the ground—to mean we are getting ready for something.

Example: Jesus said to people who wanted to follow him: *No one who puts a hand to the* ***plough*** *and looks back is fit for the kingdom of God.* [Luke chapter 9 verse 62.]

In your culture, do you have a tool for digging up the ground to get food? What do you call it?..

Talk about what Jesus meant in the Bible verse above.

POTTER

Meaning: **The person who made dishes, cups and bowls in ancient time. The potter made the dishes from clay. They dried them in the sun until they were hard.**

Sometimes we can speak of God as a potter, because God makes us.

Example: God told Jeremiah to go to the **pottery** shop:
I went there and saw the ***potter*** *making clay pots on his* ***pottery*** *wheel. And whenever the clay would not take the shape he wanted, he would change his mind and form it into some other shape. Then the Lord told me to say: "People of Israel, I, the Lord, have power over you, just as a* ***potter*** *has power over clay.* [Jeremiah chapter 18 verse 1–6.]

Talk about what it means to say that God is our **potter** and we are the clay.

POWER — SEE GOD'S POWER p 103

Praise

PRAISE

Meaning: **In the Bible, this means to worship and give glory to God.**

Example: The first Christians went to the Temple every day, but they met in their houses for the breaking of bread; they shared their food gladly; they **praised** God. [Acts chapter 2 verse 47.]

What is the word for **praise** in your language?..

PREPARATION

Meaning: **Getting ready for something.**

Examples: On the day before a big religious ceremony, the Jewish people had to get ready by making the right **preparations.**

Jesus died on the cross on the **preparation day** before the Jewish Sabbath. [John chapter 19 verse 31.]

What is the word for **preparation** in your language?..

Talk about the **preparations** you have to make before some important event happens.

PRESBYTERY

Meaning: **1 All the churches and church communities of the Uniting Church in one area which is served by the Chairperson of the presbytery. The presbytery is responsible to the Synod and the Moderator for the oversight of ministry within its particular region.**

2 Presbytery is also the name of the house where the parish priest lives (in the Catholic tradition).

SEE MODERATOR p 171 SYNOD p 255

Priest
Old Testament

PRIDE

Meaning: **Thinking that you are better or more important than other people. It is the opposite of being humble.**

Examples: *Too much* ***pride*** *will destroy you.* [Proverbs chapter 16 verse 18.]

Jesus said: *It is from within, from the human heart that evil intentions come: fornication, theft, murder, adultery, avarice, wickedness, deceit, licentiousness, envy, slander,* ***pride,*** *folly.* [Mark chapter 7 verses 21–22.]

What is the word in your language for **pride**?..

Think about how **pride** can hurt your own life.

PRIEST

Meaning: **1 In the Old Testament, a priest was the person who talked to God for the people. The priest's main job was to offer sacrifice to God. Priests were usually from the tribe of Levi.**

2 In the New Testament, all baptised Christians share in the priesthood of Jesus Christ.

3 In some Christian communities, a priest is a person chosen (ordained) to lead the church community in worship, to teach or preach about God's Word, and to give pastoral and spiritual care to the people.

4 In many churches, ordained persons are called ministers or pastors. A Minister of the Word or a Deacon are persons chosen (ordained) to lead the church community in worship, to teach or preach about God's Word, and to give pastoral and spiritual care to the people.

Examples: 1 Aaron and his sons were chosen to be **priests.** Moses anointed them with oil and put special clothes on them. [Leviticus chapter 8.]

2 *Let yourselves be built into a spiritual house, to be a holy* ***priesthood,*** *to offer spiritual sacrifices acceptable to God through Jesus Christ …*
You are a chosen race, a royal ***priesthood,*** *a holy nation, God's own people.*
[1 Peter chapter 2 verses 5, 9.]

Promised Land

PRINCE

Meaning: **A prince is the son of a king or queen.**
A prince is an important person.

Examples: In Old Testament times, the prophet Isaiah talked about the messiah who would come. He would be a **'prince of peace'.**
[Isaiah chapter 9 verse 6.]

Christians understand that Jesus Christ is the **Prince of Peace.**

PROMISED LAND

Meaning: **In the Bible story of the Israelites, we read about the Promised Land.**

The Promised Land is the land which God promised to Abraham and Sarah and their grandchildren.

Examples: Now the Lord said to Abram, 'Go from your country ... to the land that I will show you'. [Genesis chapter 12 verse 1.]

The Lord made a covenant with Abram, saying, 'To your descendants I give this land ... '. [Genesis chapter 15 verse 18.]

What is your language word for your country? ....

Talk about what land or country means to you? Does it mean the same for you as for the Israelites? Or does land have a different meaning for you?

EZEKIELS VISION
Son of man feed and be satisfied by the scroll I am giving you. I ate and it tasted as sweet as honey.

Prophet

PROPHET and PROPHECY

Meaning: **God chooses who will be a prophet.**
A prophet is someone who speaks God's message.

In the Old Testament, prophets like Moses, Isaiah and Jeremiah told the people to obey God's laws and to stop living sinful lives.

People think of those who speak out for truth and justice in our own times—such as Martin Luther King or Mahatma Gandhi—as a kind of modern day prophet.

Examples: God said to Moses: *When I want to speak to them (the people), I will choose one of them to be a* ***prophet*** *like you. I will give my message to that* ***prophet****, who will tell the people exactly what I have said.*
[Deuteronomy chapter 18 verse18.]

At that time Deborah, a ***prophetess,*** *wife of Lappidoth, was judging Israel. She used to sit under the palm of Deborah ... and the Israelites came up to her for judgment.* [Judges chapter 4 verses 4–5.]

God chose Jeremiah to be a **prophet**. Jeremiah said to God:
'I'm not a good speaker, Lord, and I'm too young.'
'Don't say you're too young,' the Lord answered. 'If I tell you to go and speak to someone, then go! And when I tell you what to say, don't leave out a word. I promise to be with you and keep you safe, so don't be afraid.' [Jeremiah chapter 1 verses 6–8.].

There was also a ***prophet,*** *Anna the daughter of Phanuel, of the tribe of Asher. ... she began to praise God and to speak about the child to all who were looking for the redemption of Jerusalem.*
[Luke chapter 2 verses 36, 38.]

Do you have anything like **prophecy** in your community? ....

Do you know anyone alive today who is a **prophet?**

PSALM 23

The good Shepherd [a]

Of David

Yahweh is my shepherd. I lack nothing. Ezk 34:1a
In grassy meadows he lets me lie. Jn 10:1–16

By tranquil streams he leads me Is 40:31
to restore my spirit. Jr 31:25
Jn 4:1a
He guides me in paths of saving justice Pr 4:11
as befits his name. 115:1

Even were I to walk in a ravine as dark as death Jb 10:21–22
I should fear no danger, for you are at my side. [b] Is 50:10
Your staff and your crook are there to soothe me.

...lament and entreaty of the innocent under per-... in thanksgiving for his rescue, vv. 22–26, and ... in the national liturgy by virtue of v. 23 and ... conclusion, vv. 27–31, where the coming of ... of God throughout the world seems to result ... ideal of the faithful servant.
...bly the first words of a familiar song. Versions ...g solace'.
'You who dwell in the sanctuary, the praise of ... Gk.
...trusted himself' versions; 'Trust yourself' Hebr.
...mouth' *hikki* conj.; Hebr. *kohi* 'my strength'.
... to hack off' *ke'ero* (from the verb *arah*) conj.; ... 'as a lion', unintelligible; Gk 'they have dug ... 'they have wounded'. • The passage recalls ... the evangelists did not make use of it in the ...ratives.
...poor life (lit. 'soul')' *'annivati* conj. Hebr. *'ani*... ...have answered me'.

h. Allusion to the messianic banquet, Is 55:1seq., rather than to the ritual meal following the communion sacrifice, Lv 3:1a.

i. 'him' versions; 'you' Hebr.

j. 'him' *'ak lo* conj.; Hebr. *'aklu* 'they have eaten'.

k. A difficult passage; it can also be interpreted 'He (the wicked) will not live, but generations will serve him'. Some MSS and the Gk have 'my soul shall live for him', an adjustment relating to belief in the resurrection.

l. 'still to come' Gk; 'they will come' Hebr.

23 a. The care of God for the upright, illustrated by two images, the shepherd, vv. 1–4, and the host of the messianic banquet, vv. 5–6.

b. 'for you are' a later addition to the text, probably to harmonise with 1 S 22:23, and to stress the allusion to David. The original text was probably: 'at my side are your crook and your staff'.

Psalm

PSALM

Meaning: **In the Old Testament there is a book of 150 poems, songs and prayers to God about different things, for example, about being happy, or sad, or in need of something. These prayers, songs and poems are called psalms.**

SEE HYMN p 121

Examples: *The Lord is my shepherd, I shall not want …* [Psalm 23.]

By the rivers of Babylon—there we sat down and there we wept when we remember Zion … [Psalm 137.]

I call upon you, O Lord, come quickly to me … [Psalm 141.]

Praise the Lord! How good it is to sing praises to our God; [Psalm 147.]

Are there songs or stories like this in your language?
Talk about some of them.

PURIFICATION

Meaning: **To make someone or something clean.**
For the Israelites, purification or being clean was a very important religious duty. They had many rules about what was clean or not clean—for food, for animals, for people, for houses. **[For example, read Leviticus chapter 11.]**

In the New Testament, Jesus said it was more important to have a clean heart, to be clean inside, to be free from sin.

Example: Jesus said: *You Pharisees and teachers are show-offs, and you're in for trouble! You wash the outside of your cups and dishes, while inside there is nothing but greed and selfishness.* [Matthew chapter 23 verse 25.]

Rabbi

R

RABBI

Meaning: **A teacher of the Jewish religion.**

Example: *Then Peter said to Jesus, **Rabbi,** it is good for us to be here.* [Mark chapter. 9 verse 5.]

Two of John's disciples saw Jesus and followed him. *When Jesus turned and saw them following, he said to them, "What are you looking for?" They said to him, "**Rabbi,** where are you staying?"* [John chapter 1 verses 37–38.]

Gamaliel was a teacher of the law. When the Jewish leaders wanted to kill Peter and the other apostles, Gamaliel warned them not to do this, because the apostles might be doing God's work. [Acts chapter 5 verses 33–39.]

What do you call teachers in your language?..

Talk about what teachers in the church do.

REAP SEE HARVEST p 109

REDEEMER

Meaning: **In the Bible, a redeemer is someone who sets people free.**

Jesus is our redeemer because He frees us from the wrong way of living by his life, his teaching, his death and his resurrection. He frees us to be sons and daughters of God.

SEE SAVIOUR p 241

Examples: God told Moses to tell the Israelites: *I am the Lord and I will free you from the … Egyptians and deliver you from slavery to them. I will **redeem** you with an outstretched arm …* [Exodus chapter 6 verse 6.]

Job had a lot of troubles and suffering, but he trusted in God to help him. He said: *I know that my **Redeemer** lives.* [Job chapter 19 verse 25.]

What is the word in your language for **redeemer**?..

Talk about times when people are **redeemed** from a curse.

Relationship

RELATIONSHIP

Meaning: **When people are part of the same family or same group they are related. They have a relationship with other members of that family or that group.**
People can also have relationships of friendship, not family.

In the Bible, God tells us we are all related because we are all daughters and sons of God.

Examples: Jesus gave us the gift to become children of God:
To all who received (Jesus), who believed in his name, he gave power to become ***children of God*** ... [John chapter 1 verse 12.]

The apostle Paul taught us: ... *All who are led by the Spirit of God are* ***children of God*** ... [Romans chapter 8 verse 14.]

How does God's love abide in anyone who has the world's goods and sees **a brother or sister** in need and yet refuses to help? [First Letter of John chapter 3 verse 17.]

They could not get married because the **relationship** was not straight: they were the wrong skin groups.

Christians everywhere have a **relationship** with each other because we are all one people together in Christ.

What is the word for **relationship** in your language? ....

Talk about right **relationships** among your people.

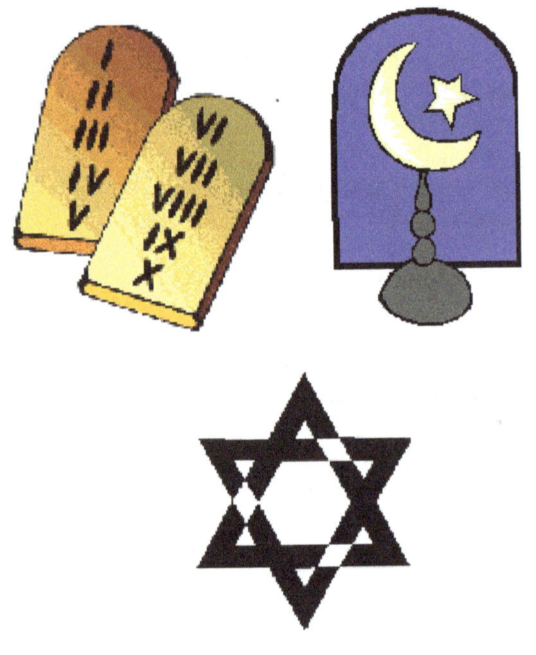

Religion

RELIGION

Meaning: **Religion is what a person thinks and believes about God, spiritual powers and the world.**
Different religions have their own beliefs and rules that tell people how to worship God and how to behave towards other people.

Examples: We believe in the **Christian religion.** This comes from what Jesus taught us about God and how to live properly.

There are other **religions** in Australia, for example, Islam and Buddhism.

If you think you are being religious but cannot control your tongue, you are fooling yourself, and everything you do is useless. ***Religion*** *that pleases God ... must be pure and spotless. You must help needy orphans and widows and not let this world make you evil.* {James chapter 1 verses 26–27.]

Is there a word like **religion** in your culture and language?..

Talk about some **religions** other than Christianity you have heard about.

REPENT - REPENTANCE

Meaning: **To be sorry for doing wrong, and to turn away from doing wrong things.**

Examples: Peter **repented** for saying he did not know Jesus after he was arrested. He went outside and cried. [Matthew chapter 26 verse 75.]

John the Baptist went around preaching to the people. He said:
Repent, *for the kingdom of heaven has come near.*
[Matthew chapter 3 verse 2.]

What is the word for **repent** in your language?..

Talk about what it feels like when you **repent** after doing something wrong.

Anglican Diocese of the Northern Territory collection

Resurrection

RESURRECTION

Meaning: **To get up in a new way from being dead. Jesus' body is changed. He will never die again. He is the start of the new creation.**

Examples: Jesus died on the cross. But three days later his followers were very surprised to find out that Jesus was alive in a new kind of way. Christians call this the **Resurrection.**

The two angels at the tomb said to the women, 'Why look among the dead for someone who is alive. Jesus is not here, **he has risen**.
[Luke chapter 24 verse 5.]

Talk about how you would explain **resurrection** to the people in your community.

REVELATION

Meaning: **Revelation is when God tells us about God's own self.**

God does this first through all the things of creation—animals, plants and people.

God also tells us about God's self through the prophets and all the books of the Bible.

Finally, God tells us best about God's self through Jesus—his words, deeds, life, death and resurrection.

Example: Long ago God spoke to our ancestors in many and various ways by the prophets, but in these last days, God has spoken to us by a Son…
[Hebrews chapter 1 verses 1–2.]

St Paul wrote:
*… surely you have already heard of … God's grace that was given me for you, and how the mystery was made known to me by **revelation** …*
[Ephesians chapter 3 verses 2–3.]

Reward

REVERENCE

Meaning: **Giving respect to God and the things of God.**

Example: God called to Moses from the burning bush. God told Moses he must show **reverence** for God. God said: Don't come any closer; take off your shoes because you are standing on holy ground.
[Exodus chapter 3 verses 4–5.]

What is the word for **reverence** in your language?...

Talk about some times and places where you want to show **reverence.**

REWARD

Meaning: **What you get for doing something good.**

Examples: The Smith family lost their favourite dog. They promised a **reward** of $50 for anyone who found it and brought it home.

If you study and work hard, your **reward** will be success.

In the New Testament, Jesus promises **rewards** to the people who follow him because of the gospel. [Mark chapter 10 verses 29–30.]

Jesus said: If anyone gives you a cup of water to drink just because you belong to Christ, then I tell you solemnly, they will certainly get their **reward.**
[Mark chapter 9 verse 41.]

What is the word for **reward** in your language?...

Have you ever received a **reward** for anything? Talk about what it felt like.

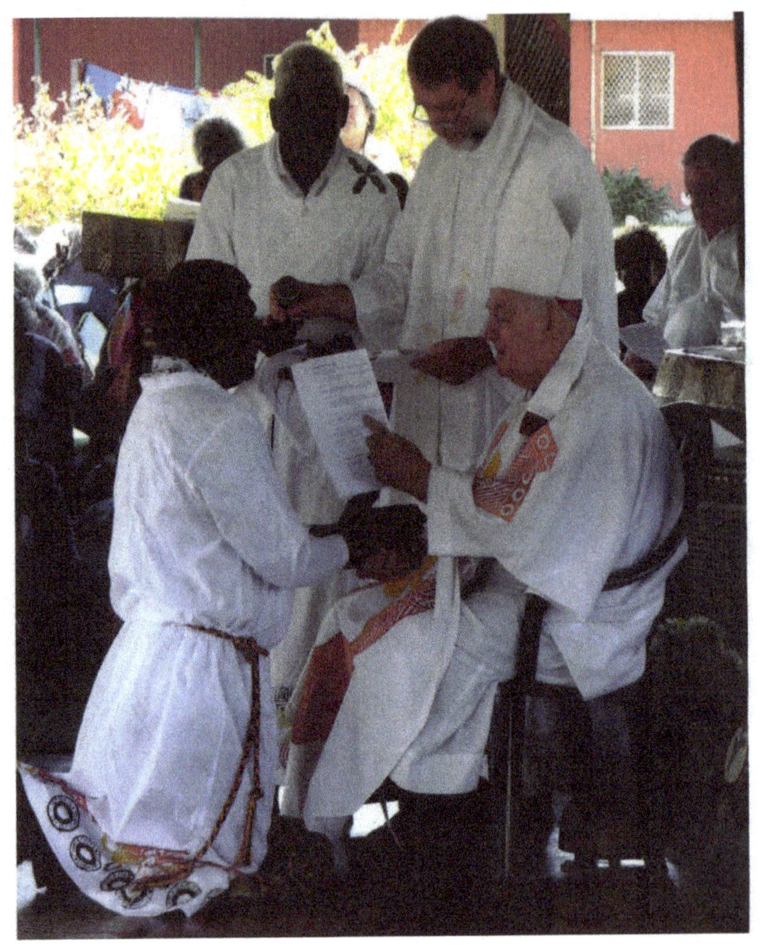

Ritual or Rite

RIGHTEOUSNESS

Meaning: **Having a right relationship with God and people.**

Living in a way that pleases God.

Examples: Jesus taught the people how to live as God wants. He said:
Blessed are the poor in spirit … blessed are those who hunger and thirst for ***righteousness****, for they will be filled …*
[Matthew chapter 5 verses 3, 6.]

The apostle Paul encouraged the people to live as God wants:
He wrote: … fasten the belt of truth around your waist and put on the breastplate of ***righteousness****.* [Ephesians chapter 6 verse 14.]

… the gospel… is the power of God for salvation to everyone who has faith, to the Jew first and also to the Greek. For in it the ***righteousness*** *of God is revealed through faith for faith; as it is written, "The one who is* ***righteous*** *will live by faith."* [Romans chapter 1 verses 16–17.]

What is the word for **righteousness** in your language?..

Talk about what it means for a Christian to be **righteous**.

RITUAL or RITE

Meaning: **The actions we do at religious ceremonies and the customs we use at church services.**

SEE CEREMONY p 41

Examples: In many churches there is a **ritual** for giving a sign of peace to other people.

Many Christians have a **ritual** of standing up to listen to the gospel.

When a person is baptised, there is a **ritual** for pouring water on their forehead or for going under the water.

Is there a word like **ritual** in your language?..

Talk about some **rituals** you have in your community.

Root of David

ROOT OF DAVID

Meaning: **This is another name, or title, for Jesus, because the family of Jesus came from King David.**

**SEE ROOT OF JESSE p 229
LION OF THE TRIBE OF JUDAH p 157**

Examples: *… the genealogy of Jesus the Messiah, the **son of David**, the son of Abraham … and Jesse the father of King David …* [Matthew chapter 1 verses 1, 6.]

*See, the Lion of the tribe of Judah, the **Root of David**, has conquered …* [Revelations chapter 5 verse 5.]

*"It is I, Jesus, who sent my angel to you … I am the **root and the descendant of David**, the bright morning star."*
[Revelations chapter 22 verse 16.]

ROOT OF JESSE SEE ROOT OF DAVID p 229

Sabbath

S

SABBATH

Meaning: **In English, we call this day of the week Saturday. This is the holy day of rest and worship for the Jewish people, and for some Christians, such as Seventh Day Adventists.**

Example: Christians observe Sunday as their **Sabbath day** because Jesus rose from the dead on that day.

Is there a word for **Sabbath** or day of rest in your language?..

Talk about what Christians do on Sunday in your church community.

SACKCLOTH

Meaning: **A very rough type of material made from goat or camel hair. It was usually a dark colour. In Old Testament times, individual people, or sometimes the whole tribe, wore sackcloth at times of great sadness or to show they were sorry.**
The Israelites often put on sackcloth at the same time as they put ashes on their heads.

Examples: When the prophet Elijah told Ahab he would be punished for doing evil, *Ahab was sorry: He tore his clothes and put* ***sackcloth*** *over his bare flesh; he fasted, lay* ***in sackcloth*** ... [1 Kings chapter 21 verse 27.]

Yahweh told Jonah to preach to the people of Nineveh, to tell them that God would soon punish them for their sins.
And the people of Nineveh believed God; they proclaimed a fast and everyone, great and small, put on ***sackcloth.***
[Jonah chapter 3 verse 5.]

Is there a word for something like **sackcloth** in your language?...

In your community, do you have special ways of showing that you are sorry when somebody dies?

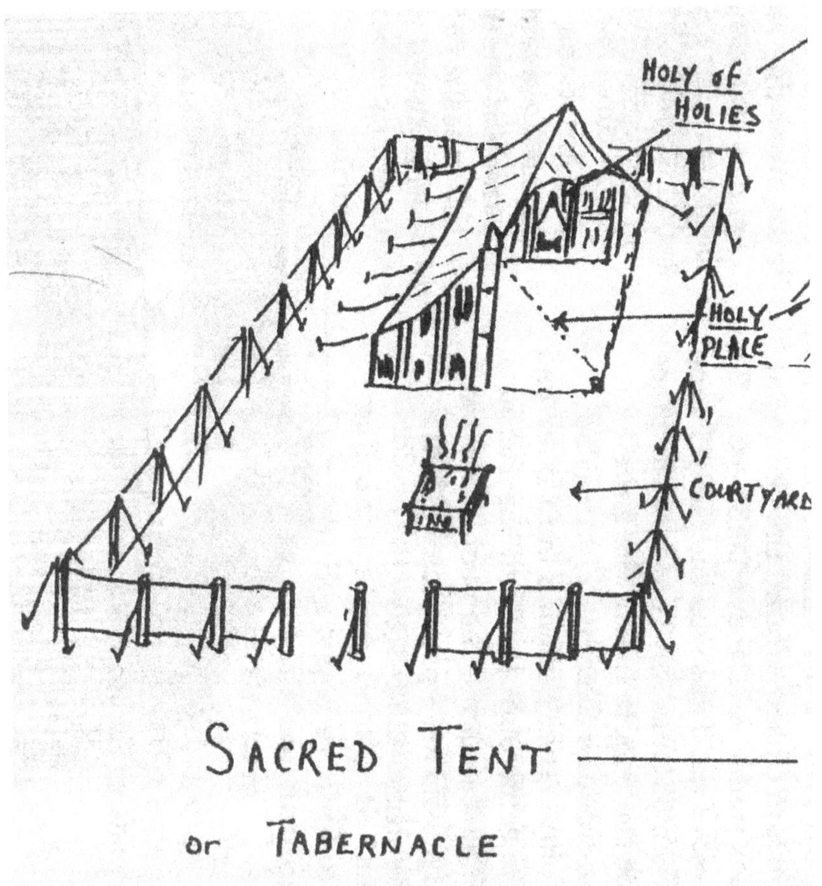

Sacred

SACRAMENT

Meaning: **A sacrament is a sign of God's action and presence in our life.**
A sacrament is an outside action of the church which we can see with an inside meaning.
The church celebrates sacraments to help us remember how much God loves us by sharing the new life of Christ with us.

Examples: We celebrate **sacraments** at special times in our lives to bring us closer to God. For example, all Christians celebrate the **Sacrament** of Baptism, which marks the beginning of our life in Jesus Christ.
[See Matthew chapter 28 verse 19.] Go ... and baptise all nations, in the name of the Father ... etc.

The outside signs of the **Sacrament** of Baptism are the water and the words spoken by the priest or minister. The inside meaning is that we belong to the Christian family in God's church.

Eucharist is another **sacrament** for Christians. Some churches have more sacraments. The Catholic Church has seven sacraments.

What **sacraments** does your church celebrate?

SACRED

Meaning: **Things, people, places or times with a special holy meaning because they are connected to God or to holy things.**

SEE HOLY p 115

Examples: There are many **sacred sites** in the country that have special meaning for Aboriginal Australians.

For Christians, a church is a **sacred** place because that is where we worship God all together.

What is the word for **sacred** in your language?..

Talk about some things that are **sacred** in your community.

Sacrifice

SACRIFICE

Meaning: **A sacrifice is something valuable a person gives up for an even more important reason.**

In the Bible, we read that the Israelites offered animals and food crops to God as a sacrifice.
They offered these sacrifices to praise and thank God, to ask God's blessing, to be in communion with God, and to make up for their sins.

SEE BURNT OFFERING p 35

Examples: Moses taught the people how to make a **sacrifice** to God. They had to take an animal from their flock, kill it, offer it to God and burn it on the altar. [Leviticus chapter 1 verses 1–9.]

Sacrifice and offering you do not desire, but you have given me an open ear. [Psalm 40 verse 6.]

For our paschal lamb, Christ, has been ***sacrificed.*** *Therefore, let us celebrate the festival, not with the old yeast ... but with the unleavened bread of sincerity and truth.* [1 Corinthians chapter 5 verses 7–8.]

SADDUCEE

Meaning: **In the time of Jesus, Sadducees were a group of Jews who followed the ancient or old Law of the Israelites. They did not believe in life after death.**

Example: Then some **Sadducees,** who say that nobody can rise from the dead, came to Jesus and asked him a question ... [Luke chapter 12 verse 18.]

Samaritan

SALVATION

Meaning: **When we are saved or rescued from something bad.**

In the Bible, God brought salvation to the Israelites when they escaped from slavery in Egypt.

In the New Testament, Jesus Christ, sent by God, brings salvation for all humanity and the whole of creation through his life, teaching, death and resurrection.

SEE REDEEMER p 217 SAVIOUR p 241

Examples: *Then Moses and the Israelites sang this song to the LORD: ...*
The LORD is my strength and my might, and ... has become my ***salvation.***
[Exodus chapter 15 verses 1–2.]

... and all flesh shall see the ***salvation*** *of God.* [Luke chapter 3 verse 6.]

Is there a word for **salvation** in your language? ....

Have you ever been saved from something bad? Talk about your experience.

SAMARITAN

Meaning: **A person who lived in Samaria. That is the country north of Judaea in the time of Jesus. Jewish people and Samaritan people did not agree about some religious ideas, so there was conflict between them.**

Example: The **Samaritan** woman said to Jesus: What? You are a Jew and you ask me, a **Samaritan**, for a drink?
Jews in fact do not talk to **Samaritans.** [John chapter 4 verse 9.]

Read the story of the **Good Samaritan** in Luke chapter 10 verses 25–37.

Do you know any people in your community like the **Good Samaritan**?

Sanhedrin

SANCTIFICATION

Meaning: **To make a thing or person holy or sacred for God by taking away sinfulness.**
This can happen when a person says 'Sorry' for sins.

Example: Let me put it like this: if you are guided by the Spirit, you will be in no danger of [sinful behaviour] ... What the Spirit brings is very different: love, joy, peace, patience, kindness, goodness, trustfulness, gentleness and self-control. [Galatians chapter 5 verses 16, 22.]

Do you not know that wrongdoers will not inherit the kingdom of God? ... And this is what some of you used to be. But you were washed, you were ***sanctified,*** *you were justified in the name of the Lord Jesus Christ and in the Spirit of our God.* [1 Corinthians chapter 6 verses 9, 11.]

What is a word like **sanctification** in your language?..

Talk about what **sanctification** means for your Christian life – what does it mean to live a holy life.

SANHEDRIN

Meaning: **The name for the high council of leaders of the Jewish community. The council was made up of 71 elders.**

Example: When the soldiers arrested Jesus they took him to the high priest and the other elders. They asked him questions. The chief priests and the whole **Sanhedrin** were looking for evidence against Jesus, even if it was not true, so they could pass the death sentence on him. [Matthew chapter 26 verses 57-59.]

What is the word for the high group of elders in your community?...................................

Talk about what a high elder in your community does.

SATAN SEE DEMON p 69

Scribes

SAVIOUR

Meaning: **Someone who saves or rescues a person from death or danger. In the Old Testament, the Israelites called God their saviour. In the New Testament, Christians call Jesus their Saviour.**

SEE REDEEMER p 217

Examples: God told the Israelites not to be afraid:
When you pass through the waters, I will be with you; and through rivers, they shall not [drown] you; when you walk through fire you shall not be burned … for I am the Lord your God, the Holy One of Israel, your ***Saviour.*** [Isaiah chapter 43 verses 2–3.]

When Jesus went to stay with the Samaritans, he taught them many things about God and about how to live. The Samaritans said: Now we know that he really is the **saviour** of the world. [John chapter 4 verses 41–423.]

For the grace of God has appeared, bringing salvation to all … we wait for the blessed hope and the manifestation of the glory of our great God and ***Saviour, Jesus Christ****.* [Titus chapter 2 verses 11, 13.]

Is there a word like **saviour** in your language?..

Talk about how the teaching and life of Jesus our **saviour** helps us to live better lives.

SCRIBES

Meaning: **Learned Jewish officials. Their job was to pass on knowledge of the Jewish Law. They often spoke against Jesus.**

Example: *As Jesus was walking in the Temple, the chief priests,* ***the scribes*** *and the elders came to him and said, 'By what authority are you doing these things? Who gave you this authority to do them'?*
[Mark chapter 11 verses 27–28.]

Scroll

SCROLL

Meaning: **A roll of paper with writing on it. In the time of Jesus, scrolls were made of papyrus, a kind of paper the Egyptians used.**

Example: The apostle John had a vision. He wrote it in the book of Revelation:
In the right hand of the one sitting on the throne, I saw a ***scroll*** *that had writing on the inside and on the outside. And it was sealed in seven places. I saw a mighty angel ask with a loud voice, "Who is worthy to open the* ***scroll*** *and break the seals?"* [Revelation chapter 5 verses 1–2.]

Have you ever seen a **scroll**? Talk about what they are used for today?

SEAL

Meaning: **In everyday life, to close up a letter in an envelope by folding down the sticky flap.**

In Old Testament times, a small piece of stone with a special name or mark on it. To close up an important message, they folded the paper, put soft wax over the join and pressed the stone seal onto it.

Example: The apostle John had a vision. He wrote it in the book of Revelation:
In the right hand of the one sitting on the throne, I saw a scroll that had writing on the inside and on the outside. And it was ***sealed*** *in seven places. I saw a mighty angel ask with a loud voice, "Who is worthy to open the scroll and break the* ***seals****?"* [Revelation chapter 5 verses 1–2.]

SERPENT

Meaning: **Another word for a snake.**

SEE SNAKE p 249

Shepherd

SHEPHERD

Meaning: **In New Testament times, a person who looks after the sheep and goats when they go out to eat grass. The shepherd keeps the sheep and goats safe from wild animals like lions or wolves.**

Examples: You, Lord, are my **shepherd.** I will never be in need.
You let me rest in fields of green grass.
You lead me to streams of peaceful water, and you refresh my life.
[Psalm 23 verses 103.]

In the New Testament, Jesus is like a **shepherd** for his followers:
I am the **good shepherd**; I know my own and my own know me.
[John chapter 10 verse 14.]

Do you know any leaders today who are like **good shepherds**? Talk about how they care for the people.

SHIELD

Meaning: **In times long ago, a piece of wood or steel held in front of the body to stop getting hit by the spears of the enemy.**

Examples: In the Bible, God is like a **shield** protecting all God's people.
The Word of the LORD *came to Abram in a vision, "Do not be afraid, Abram, I am your **shield** ...* [Genesis chapter 15 verse 1.]

For Christians, our faith is like a **shield** to keep us safe from evil.
[Ephesians, chapter 6 verse 16.]

What is the word for **shield** in your language?..

Talk about how the **shield** was used in your community in times past.

Sign

SIGN

Meaning: **A thing, something we can see, which reminds us of something without using words.**

Examples: When we see footprints in the sand, that is a **sign** that someone has walked there.

In the Bible, after the Great Flood, God made the rainbow a **sign** of God's Covenant with Noah and the human race.
[Genesis chapter 9 verses 12–13.]

*Then the cloud covered the tent of meeting and the glory of the LORD filled the tabernacle … For the **cloud** of the LORD was on the tabernacle by day, and **fire** was in the cloud by night, before the eyes of all the house of Israel at each stage of their journey.* [Exodus chapter 40 verses 34, 38.] The cloud and the fire were **signs** that God was with them.

Is there a word for **sign** in your language? ……………………………………………………...

Talk about some of the **signs** in our everyday life and what they mean. What are some of the **signs** in the Bible?

SIN

Meaning: **When we know something is wrong but we still do it, that is sin.**

The Bible tells us that sin means we do something bad against other people or against God, instead of loving them.

Example: The prodigal son, when he was sorry for doing wrong, came home to his father and said, 'Father, I have **sinned** against God and against you. [See Luke chapter 15 verse 11.]

*For there is no distinction, since all have **sinned** and fall short of the glory of God; they are now justified by God's grace as a gift, through the redemption that is in Christ Jesus.* [Romans chapter 3 verses 23–24.]

Is there a word for **sin** in your language? ………………………………………………………

Everyone knows that **sin** hurts people. Talk about how this happens.

Slave

SLAVE

Meaning: **A person without any freedom who is owned by someone else. The slave has to work for that person for nothing.**

Examples: In the Bible, a lot of people owned **slaves** who worked for them. They did not understand then that treating people like **slaves** was wrong.

When King Solomon went to war and beat the tribes around him, he made those people into **slaves** to work for him. [1 Kings chapter 9 verses 20–21.]

Paul wrote a letter to Philemon and told him that he must not treat Onesimus as a **slave** any more but as a dear brother. [Philemon verses 15–16.]

Do you know of any places where there are **slaves** today?

SNAKE

Meaning: **In the Bible, a snake is a sign for different things. In the bible, it is often called a 'serpent'.**

SEE SERPENT p 243

Examples: In the story of the beginning of the world, the **snake** is a sign for the devil and evil. The **snake** told Adam and Eve to disobey God.
[Genesis chapter 3 verses 1–14.]

When the Israelites walked through the desert, the **snake** was a sign for both death and healing. **Snakes** bit some people and they died. But Moses told them to make a **bronze snake** and put it up on a stick. Anyone bitten by a **snake** could look at the **bronze snake** and they would live. [Number chapter 21 verses 4–9.]

What are some names for **serpents** or **snakes** in your community?....................................

Talk about what the **snake** means in the bible.

Son of Man

SON OF GOD

Meaning: **When we say Jesus is Son of God, we mean that he comes from God the Father to be with us. He is the second person of the Trinity. He enables us to become adopted daughters and sons of God.**

SEE TRINITY p 269

Example: *The angel said to (Mary), "The Holy Spirit will come upon you, and the power of the Most High will overshadow you; therefore the child to be born will be holy; he will be called **Son of God**.* [Luke chapter 1 verse 35.]

John the Baptist said: *I myself have seen and have testified that this (Jesus) is the **Son of God**.* [John chapter 1 verse 34.]

*Martha said to Jesus, "Yes, Lord I believe that you are the Messiah, the **Son of God**, the one coming into the world."* [John chapter 11 verse 27.]

After Jesus died on the cross, there was an earthquake. The soldier and others guarding Jesus were terrified. They said:
*This man was really **God's son.*** Matthew chapter 27 verse 54.]

SON OF MAN

Meaning: **Son of Man is another way of talking about a human being. When we talk about Jesus like this, it sometimes means he is a very special person who does the work of God.**

Example: *Then Jesus said to (Zaccheus), "Today salvation has come to this house, because he too is a son of Abraham. For the **Son of Man** came to seek out and to save the lost.* [Luke chapter 19 verses 9–10.]

When Jesus came to the region of Caesarea Philippi he put this question to his disciples, 'Who do people say the **Son of Man** is?' (That means, 'Who do people say that I am?') [Matthew chapter 16 verse 13.]

SORCERY SEE MAGIC p 163

Spirit

SPIRIT

Meaning: **1 In the Bible, sometimes this means the power of God that we can't see, but is all around us, giving life to everything.**

2 Sometimes spirit means the Holy Spirit. The Holy Spirit is given to us after Jesus died and rose from the dead.

3 Sometimes it means the inside life of a person that we cannot see.

SEE HOLY SPIRIT p 117

Example: 1 The Psalmist said: Where could I go to escape your **spirit**? Where could I flee from your presence? You are everywhere … [Psalm139 verse 7.]

After Jesus was baptised in the River Jordan, the **Spirit** sent him out into the desert to fast for forty days. [Mark chapter 1 verses 12–13.}

2 When the day of Pentecost came around, the disciples were together in a room. They heard the sound of a strong wind, and they were all filled with the **Holy Spirit**. [Acts chapter 2 verses 1–4.]

3 *The child (Jesus) grew and became strong in* ***spirit.*** [Luke chapter 1 verse 80.]

At once Jesus perceived in his ***spirit*** *that they were discussing these questions among themselves* … [Mark chapter 2 verse 8.]

What are some words for **spirit** in your language?..

SPIRITUALITY

Meaning: **The way a person tries to grow to become their truest and best self, freely loving and serving other people. Christian spirituality is doing this in the way Jesus taught us, with the help of the Holy Spirit.**

Examples: In the Gospels, we can learn about the **spirituality of Jesus**. We can learn how he thought and acted towards God and people. He is the model for Christians.

When a person turns to Jesus, their **spirituality** changes.

Talk about what helps your **spiritual life** to grow.

UNITING HOUSE
UNITING CHURCH IN AUSTRALIA
NORTHERN SYNOD
NORTHERN REGIONAL COUNCIL OF U.A.I.C.C
and
ABORIGINAL RESOURCE AND DEVELOPMENT SERVICES INC.
Entry from Railway Street

Synod

SYNAGOGUE

Meaning: **At first a gathering of Jewish people. Later, a synagogue was a building or place where Jewish people could meet to worship God when they could not worship in the Jerusalem temple.**

Examples: *When (Jesus) came to Nazareth, where he had been brought up, he went to the* ***synagogue*** *on the Sabbath day, as was his custom.* [Luke chapter 4 verse 16.]

A Jew called Apollos from Alexandria came to Ephesus. He was full of enthusiasm about Jesus.
He began to speak boldly in the ***synagogue****; but when Priscilla and Aquila heard him, they took him aside and explained the Way of God to him more accurately.* [Acts chapter 18 verse 26.]

Is there a **synagogue** in Darwin? Where is it?

SYNOD

Meaning: **All the churches and church communities of the Uniting Church in a large area, usually a state, served by the Moderator. A synod is made of a number of smaller areas called presbyteries.**

SEE DIOCESE p 71

Example: The Moderator has the pastoral and administrative care of all the churches and church communities that belong to the **Synod.**

Who is the Moderator of the Uniting Church in the **Synod** where you live?

Tax

T

TABERNACLE

Meaning: **When the Israelites were in the desert after they left Egypt, the tabernacle was the special tent where they worshipped God living among them ... [Exodus chapter 25 verse 8.]**

In some Christian churches, the tabernacle is the small, closed space on or near the altar where the Eucharist (Blessed Sacrament) is kept.

Example: God told the Israelites that they were to follow a special pattern in making the **tabernacle.** (Ex 25:9)

Talk about the places where you find God especially present.

TAX

Meaning: **The money you have to give to the government from the money you get from working. The government uses it to pay for things like roads, schools, hospitals, and the army.**

Examples: When Jesus lived in Palestine, the Romans were the big bosses. They made the Jews pay **taxes** to their top boss who was called Caesar. One day the Jews asked Jesus: Is it OK to pay **taxes** to Caesar?
[Matthew chapter 22 verse 17.]

The Jews also had to pay a **tax** to the temple to keep it repaired. [Matthew chapter 17 verse 24.]

Talk about how the government uses the people's **tax.**

For the Jewish people
the temple in Jerusalem
was the most holy place

TEMPLE

Meaning: **A building where people gather to worship God. For the Jewish people, the Jerusalem Temple was the most holy place because it was the sign of God's presence with them.**

Example: The prophet Anna 'never left the **Temple**, serving God day and night with fasting and prayer.' [Luke chapter 2 verse 37.]

Do you not know that you are **God's temple** and that God's Spirit dwells in you? If anyone destroys **God's temple**, God will destroy that person. For **God's temple** is holy, and you are that **temple.**
[1 Corinthians chapter 3 verses 16-17.]

Is there a word in your language for a place where people worship God or where God is believed to be specially present? ....

Talk about a time when you have felt that God was with you.

TEMPTATION

Meaning 1: **In everyday life, to feel very strongly that you want to do something bad.**

Example 1: It was a big **temptation** for those people to steal the money on the table. But they said, no, it would be wrong: "We will not take it."

Even if you think you can stand up to **temptation,** be careful not to fall. You are **tempted** in the same way that everyone else is **tempted.** But God can be trusted not to let you be **tempted** too much …
[1 Corinthians chapter 10 verses 12–13.]

Meaning 2: **In the Bible, temptation can mean a test to see if a person will be faithful.**
God does not tempt people to do wrong things.

Example 2: In the story about Abraham and Isaac, God tested Abraham's faith in God. Abraham didn't want to kill Isaac. But because he thought God wanted that, he was ready to kill Isaac. But when God saw that Abraham was faithful, God stopped him from killing Isaac. [Genesis 22 verses 1–9.]

What is the word for **temptation** in your language?...........................
Talk about some times you have felt **temptation,** or some times when your faithfulness to God was tested.

Ten Commandments

TEN COMMANDMENTS

Meaning: **The ten laws which God gave to the people through Moses.**

The 'ten commandments' means the laws God gave to Moses on Mt. Sinai. Moses had to write them down on the tablet.

Example: Yahweh said to Moses, 'Come up to me on the mountain and stay there while I give you the stone tablets—the law and the **commandments** ... [Exodus chapter 24 verse 12]

Does your culture have laws like the **Ten Commandments**?.......................................

Talk about where the laws came from.

TENT

Meaning: **These days, a canvas shelter for living in when you go camping in the bush. It is propped up with poles.**

SEE TABERNACLE p 257

Example: The Israelites used to live in **tents** in the desert. Their **tents** were often made of goat skins.

What is the word in your language for a shelter in the bush where some people live?
....

TENT OF THE LORD'S PRESENCE

Meaning: **The special tent outside the camp where Moses used to talk and listen to God. Sometimes it was called the Tent of Meeting. [Exodus chapter 33 verses 7–8.]**

SEE TABERNACLE p 257

Example: Moses used to take the **tent** and pitch it outside the camp ... He called it the **Tent of Meeting**. Anyone who had to ask Yahweh about something would go out to the **Tent of Meeting**. [Exodus chapter 33 verses 7–8.]

Throne

TESTIMONY

Meaning: **What you say to show that something is true. A person who knows what happened or saw something testifies or gives testimony about it. A person who gives that testimony is called a witness.**

Examples: The apostle John wrote that he was telling people what he knew:
... what we have heard, what we have seen with our eyes, what we have looked at and touched with our hands, concerning the word of life — this life was revealed, and we have seen it and ***testify*** *to it ...*
[First Letter of John chapter 1 verses 1–2.]

If we receive human ***testimony****, the* ***testimony*** *of God is greater ...*
And this is the ***testimony:*** *God gave us eternal life, and this life is in [God's] son.* [First Letter of John chapter 5 verses 9, 11.]

THEOLOGY

Meaning: **The study of things to do with God. Believers who want to understand more about what they believe study theology.**

Example: Students at *Nungalinya* College can study **theology,** scripture and aspects of Church ministry.

Talk about how you came to study **theology.**

THRONE

Meaning: **A special chair that the king or queen or some other very important person sits on.**

Examples: God told the Prophet Nathan to tell King David he would have an important descendant:
I will raise up your offspring after you ... and I will establish his kingdom. He shall build a house for my name, and I will establish the ***throne*** *of his kingdom forever.* [2 Samuel chapter 7 verses 12–13.]

The apostle John had a vision of the future:
At once I was in the spirit, and there in heaven stood a ***throne****, with one seated on the* ***throne****! ... around the* ***throne*** *... are four living creatures ... and the living creatures give glory and honour and thanks to the one who is seated on the* ***throne****, who lives forever and ever ...* [Revelation chapter 4 verses 2, 6, 9.]

Do the elders in your community sit in a special place?

M & L Joshua

Tongues

TITHE

Meaning: **One tenth of a person's money or income. If you have $100, then $10 is one tenth or a tithe. It was the money the Israelites gave to God at the temple.**

Example: Many people these days give a **tithe** to God through the Church or to help poor people. Pat earned $200 and gave $20 to the church or to the poor.

TONGUES

Meaning: **In the Bible, speaking or singing in tongues is one of the gifts of the Holy Spirit.**
When people pray using the gift of tongues, they pray straight from their heart, sometimes using unusual words and sounds.
The everyday meaning of tongues is languages.

SEE GIFTS OF THE SPIRIT p 97

Examples: Sometimes if you go to a prayer or fellowship meeting, you can hear people praying in **tongues.**

There are many different gifts but always the same Spirit. ... One person may have the gift of preaching with wisdom, someone else may have the gift of healing ... another person may have the **gift of tongues ...** [Read 1Corinthians chapter 12 verses 4–11.].]

Have you ever heard people praying **in tongues**? Talk about your experiences.

TORAH

Meaning: **Torah is a Hebrew word that means teaching or instruction. Jewish people call the first five books of the bible (the Pentateuch), the Torah.**

SEE LAW p 149 PENTATEUCH p 197

Example: In the **Torah** (the Books of Genesis, Exodus, Leviticus, Numbers and Deuteronomy), there are many stories, songs and genealogies, as well as laws, that taught the people how to live.

What is the word for law in your language? ....

Talk about some story or song in your law that teaches people how to live well.

Transfiguration

TRADITION

Meaning: **What parents teach their children and grandchildren.**

In the church, tradition is the Christian faith passed on to us from the past - the Bible, prayer and worship customs, ways of doing things, church teachings and so on. We pass this tradition on to our children and their children.

Example: Aboriginal old people pass on their **traditions** to their communities. The church also passes on its **traditions** to the Christian community of believers.

Is there a word or an idea like **tradition** in your community?.......................................

Talk about who passed on the Christian **tradition** to you? To whom will you pass it on?

TRANSFIGURATION

Meaning: **A big change in what someone or something looks like.**

In the Bible, transfiguration means the way Jesus looked very different when he prayed to God on the mountain top.
[Luke chapter 9 verses 28–36.]

Example: Jesus took Peter and James and his brother John and led them up a high mountain. There in their presence, he was **transfigured**: his face shone like the sun and his clothes became as white as the light.
[Matthew chapter 17 verses 1–3.]

Is there a word or an idea like **transfiguration** in your language?.....................................

Truth

TRINITY

Meaning: **Trinity is the name Christians give to the One God revealed to us in three persons as Father, Son and Holy Spirit.**

We know Jesus as the Son sent by God the Father and we know the Holy Spirit as new life from God. The Son is true God. The Holy Spirit is true God. But God is One God, not three Gods. God is a communion in love.

Example: And when **Jesus** had been baptised, just as he came up from the water, suddenly the heavens were opened to him and he saw the **Spirit of God** descending like a dove and alighting on him. And a **voice from heaven** said, **"This is my Son, the Beloved**," with whom I am well pleased.
[Matthew chapter 3 verses 16–17.]

TRUTH

Meaning: **What is true or correct. The facts about something.**

In the Bible, truth means the correct way to live as God taught us.
When Jesus Christ came, he taught us more about God's truth and how we are to live.

Examples: It is the **truth** that the sun rises in the east and sets in the west.

*The law indeed was given through Moses; grace and **truth** came through Jesus Christ.* [John chapter 1 verse 17.]

Jesus taught us **truth** in the way that he lived. He said:
*I am the way, and **the truth** and the life.* [John chapter 14 verse 6.]

Jesus said to his followers that if they would keep on listening to his words and obeying them, they would truly be his disciples:
*...you will know the **truth** and the **truth** will make you free.*
[John chapter 8 verses 31–32.]

What is the word or idea for **truth** in your language?...

Unclean

U

UNCLEAN

Meaning: **The Israelites had very strict religious rules about what was clean or not clean about food, animals or people.**
Some animals were unclean and some sicknesses made people unclean. [Leviticus chapter 11.]

SEE PURIFICATION p 215

Examples: Moses taught the people what animals they were allowed to eat and what animals they could not eat:
Of their flesh you shall not eat, and their carcasses you shall not touch; they are ***unclean*** *for you.* [Leviticus chapter 11 verse 8.]

But Jesus taught the people that only bad things in a person's heart make a person **unclean.** [Matthew chapter 23 verses 25–26.]

When the apostle Peter was in Joppa, he had a vision. In the vision, God taught him that everyone and everything that God has made are clean. There are no **unclean** animals or people. [Acts chapter 10 verses 9–16.]

UNLEAVENED BREAD

Meaning: **Bread made without yeast, so that it does not rise up.**

Examples: According to their stories, when the Israelites got out of Egypt, they left in such a hurry that the women did not have time to put the yeast in the bread. They remembered this at the festival of **Unleavened Bread**.

This day shall be a day of remembrance for you. You shall celebrate it as a festival to the Lord … Seven days you shall eat ***unleavened bread****.*
[Exodus chapter 12 verses 14.15.]

Do you have anything like **unleavened bread** in your community?...................................

Talk about how you make damper.

Veil or Curtain

V

VEIL or CURTAIN

Meaning: **A piece of cloth that covers something or someone's head.**
The curtain in the temple.
A veil is sometimes called a curtain.

Examples: When Rebecca saw Isaac coming, she put her **veil** over her face.
Then she got married to Isaac. [Genesis chapter 24 verses 64–65.]

The inside part of the Jewish temple, called the Holy of Holies, had a curtain or **veil** to cover it over.
When Jesus died on the cross, the **veil of the Temple** was torn in two from top to bottom. [Matthew chapter 27 verse 51.]

Are there ceremony places in your country where only high ceremony men and women can go?

Is there a name for those places?..

What does it mean that the temple **curtain** was torn when Jesus died?

VICTORY

Meaning: **To win a game in sport.**
To win a fight in war.
To win in beating a problem.

Examples: The Wanderers team won a **victory** in the football game last week.

Jesus Christ has won a **victory** over death?

What is the word in your language for **victory** in a game?...

Talk about a famous **victory** in the Bible (eg David and Goliath.)

Vision

VISION

Meaning: **A special kind of seeing that some prophets have—they can see in their mind what other people cannot see. Sometimes this means they can see what will happen in the future.**

Sometimes vision can mean a goal or good thing we would like to see happen.

Examples: In the Book of Revelation in the Bible we can read about the **vision** given by the Spirit to John.

When Paul was travelling to Damascus, he had a **vision.** He fell off his horse and heard a voice saying, Saul, Saul, why are you persecuting me? [Acts of the Apostles chapter 9 verses 3–9.]

Do you have a **vision** for yourself about what you would like to happen in the future?...

Do you know of any people in your community who can see **visions** that other people cannot see? Talk about it.

VOW

Meaning: **A promise you make to God.**

Example: Hannah was very sad because she could not have a child. She made a **vow** to God that if God gave her a boy child, she would give that child to serve God all his life. [1 Samuel chapter 1 verses 9–11.]

Is there a word like **vow** in your language?...

Talk about what it means to keep a **vow** you have made to God?

Wealth

W

WEALTH or TREASURE

Meaning: **A lot of valuable things—money, houses, jewellery, cars. A rich person has a lot of wealth.**

In the Bible, wealth was having a lot of cattle or sheep.

Wealth also means having a lot of children, or a good education, good health and good friends.

Examples: The rich young man wanted to follow Jesus. Jesus told him he must first sell everything and give his money to the poor. The rich young man was sad because he did not want to give away his **wealth**.
[Matthew chapter 19 verses 16–22.]

*Jesus taught his disciples: Do not store up for yourselves **treasures** on earth ... but store up for yourselves **treasures** in heaven.* [Matthew chapter 6 verses 19–20.]

What is the word for **wealth** in your language?..

Talk about what you think **wealth** is.

WONDERS

Meaning: **In the Bible, signs and miracles that happen.**

SEE MIRACLES p 171

Example: Jesus did many **wonders** among the people. The first **wonder** or sign he did was at Cana when he turned the water into wine. After this his followers believed in him. [John chapter 2 verses 1–11.]

What is the word for **wonder** in your language?..

Talk about **wonders** you have seen in your life.

Words <u>written</u> on paper with pen

WORSHIP

Meaning: **When we make God the most important one, or 'high one' in our lives and Church ceremonies and thank God for everything.**

Examples: In the Bible, King Nebuchadnezzar told the three young men they must **worship** the golden statue or be thrown into the fire.
They refused—they would only **worship** God. [Daniel 3]

When we pray and sing songs in church, we **worship** God.

What word is used for **worship** in your language?.............................

Talk about the ways people like to **worship** God.

WRITTEN

Meaning: **Words and ideas not spoken with the mouth, but written on paper with a pen or pencil.**

SEE ORAL p 187

Examples: The books of the Bible were **written** a long time ago.

When Jesus went to the synagogue on the Sabbath, he opened the book and found the place where it was **written:**
The Lord's spirit has come to me ... and chosen me to tell the good news to the poor. [Luke chapter 4 verses 17–18.]

Talk about some of the things **written** in your language.

Yoke

YAHWEH

Meaning: **The holy name for God used by the Israelites. In English language bibles, instead of Yahweh, the word LORD is used.**

Examples: In the Bible, when Moses asked what was God's name, God said, "I am who I am". [Exodus chapter 3 verse14.]
This means the same as **Yahweh.**

When Moses came down from Mt Sinai, he told the Israelites what laws **Yahweh** had given them.

What is the word for God in your language? ....

Talk about some different names for God that we use.

YOKE

Meaning: **A thing put around the head or neck of an animal and joined to a cart so that it could pull heavy loads.**

A yoke was also a picture for the idea of being led along by God's Will.

Example: Jesus said, Come to me all you who labour and are overburdened, and I will give you rest ... My **yoke** is easy and my burden is light.
[Matthew chapter 11 verses 28–30.]

Talk about what you think Jesus meant by saying "my **yoke** is easy".

Zion

Z

ZEALOTS

Meaning: **The name for a group of Jews who wanted to fight to get rid of the Romans as rulers of Palestine.**

Example: One of the 12 that Jesus chose as a follower was Simon, who had been a **Zealot**. [Luke chapter 6 verse 15]

ZION

Meaning: **Another name for Jerusalem.**

Example: David captured the fortress of **Zion,** that is, the Citadel of David (in Jerusalem). [2 Samuel chapter 5 verse 7.]

CPSIA information can be obtained
at www.ICGtesting.com
Printed in the USA
FSHW02n2346010618
48747FS

9 781920 691936